SOUTHWESTERN INDIAN CEREMONIALS

by TOM BAHTI

The late Tom Bahti, a graduate of the Anthropology Department of the University of New Mexico, was for many years a dealer and collector of Indian art in his Tucson shop, now operated by his son Mark. Nationally recognized as an authority on the arts and crafts of the southwestern Indians, he judged numerous exhibits, wrote many articles, and lectured widely on the subject.

Mr. Bahti's interest in Indians was not limited to their arts and crafts. During his lifetime he actively participated in several organizations which sought to improve the welfare of Indians through self-help programs. He was a friend to them and strongly believed in their causes.

Mr. Bahti is also the author of *Southwestern Indian Arts and Crafts* and *Southwestern Indian Tribes*.

The ceremonies described are limited to those which a casual visitor to the Southwest might have the good fortune to see. They represent only a fraction of the ceremonials performed by southwestern Indian tribes.

1982 revision by Mark Bahti

Hopi paho *or prayer stick*

Photography and Book Design by K. C. DenDooven

Seventh Printing, 1990

SOUTHWESTERN INDIAN CEREMONIALS. COPYRIGHTED 1970 BY KC PUBLICATIONS, INC.
LC 79-136004 · ISBN: 0-916122-02-6

Introduction

Religion has been described as man's attempt to control those forces which lie beyond the glow of his campfire and it matters little whether the reference is made to a small band of hunters huddled in a cave around a cooking fire or a modern city dweller who cringes before the prospect of a nuclear fireball destroying his modern metropolis. The basic need is identical.

When discussing religion, either one's own or someone else's, it is best not to be too concerned with logic, for all mythology, whether based on written or spoken traditions, is singularly illogical. A Christian, for example, may find no inconsistency in his acceptance of the Commandment "thou shalt not kill", along with capital punishment, armies (and the chaplains who serve them), germ warfare and nuclear weapons, but the rationalization for this is based not on logic but on an unquestioning belief in the myths of his own society. In examining the religion of another society, however, he may not be as tolerant and is either indignant or condescendingly amused if all beliefs cannot be neatly and logically pigeonholed into an instantly comprehensive concept.

Further complications arise with the tremendous variation in understanding and degree of belief among the members of any religious sect. The range of belief extends from the fanatically devout to the passively indifferent in all groups. It is less accurate to say, "All Christians believe that . . ." than to say, "Most (or some) Christians believe that . . ."

Attempts to translate religious concepts from one language to another cause additional confusion; there is no equivalent in the English vocabulary, for example, for the Zuni word koko or the Hopi word kachina. Conversely the Zunis have no equivalent for the English word religion; they regard religion as being inseparable from life itself.

The brief descriptions which follow are not intended to present Southwestern Indian ceremonials as "peculiar" or "quaintly colorful" but simply as accounts of attempts by fellow human beings to meet a basic need in ways which are merely different from our own.

Superstition, it should be recalled, is the other man's religion.

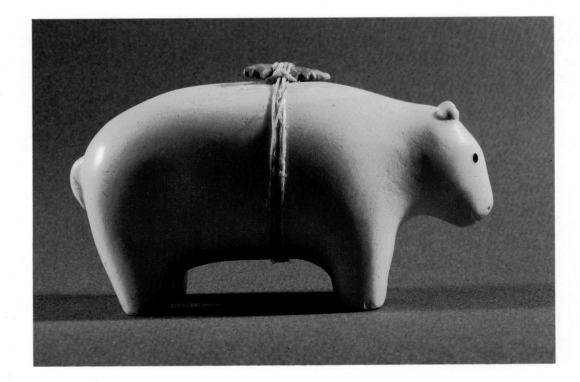

Native Religions and Foreign Influences

That native ceremonies are still performed by the Indians of the Southwest is a tribute to their way of life and the strength of their religious beliefs.

From prehistoric times to the present it has been customary for the various tribes in the Southwest to borrow from each other's religion. If one group performed a particularly effective ceremony, it could be learned from them and performed as one's own. Dances, songs and rituals were shared freely and the practice continues today.

It was not uncommon for even traditional enemies to borrow each other's ceremonials. Much of Navajo mythology and their use of sandpainting, for example, was adapted from Pueblo tribes, and the Hopi possess a number of kachinas they recognize as being of Navajo origin. The similarities in the emergence myths of many Southwestern tribes indicate a sharing of legends also.

No group presumed its religion to be superior to that of another and certainly no tribe ever conducted warfare against another for the purpose of forcing its religious beliefs upon them.

It must have been bewildering, therefore, to find that the European invaders of the Southwest made a special effort to stamp out native beliefs in order to impose their own religious doctrines.

The Spaniards explored, conquered and settled the Southwest to harvest gold for the Crown and souls for the Church. Civil and church authorities regarded the native people as barbarians, completely devoid of civilization, government and religion. They saw native ceremonies not as expressions of religious faith but as mere "idolatries." They felt a duty to teach the savages civilization and Christianity. It was not a matter of replacing one culture with another since they didn't believe the Indian had a culture to begin with.

Nevertheless, this is exactly what they proceeded to do. The destruction of kachina masks and religious paraphernalia was carried out whenever possible. "Idolaters" were confined in stocks and flogging was a common punishment used to enforce the Spanish prohibition of Indian cermonies. But instead of stamping out native rituals they merely drove them underground. Several minor rebellions and the Great Pueblo Revolt of 1680 are directly traceable to the harsh punishment meted out to religious leaders.

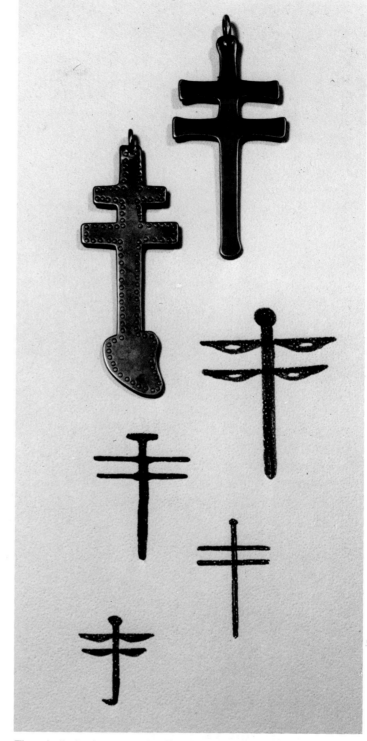

The similarity between the Franciscan's double barred Cross of Caravaca and the dragon fly designs used on Pueblo pottery resulted in the ready acceptance among Southwestern tribes of this religious symbol for non-religious reasons. The motif at the base of the brass cross on the left represents the sacred heart or fifth wound of Christ.

The Church finally learned to live side by side with native religion though it is doubtful whether it ever was—or is—as tolerant of Indian religion as the Indian is of Western religion.

The American invasion of the Southwest, which followed the Treaty of Guadalupe Hidalgo in 1848, had no immediate effect on native religions. Catholic missions continued to operate and the Pueblo Indians made nominal use of them while adhering to native beliefs.

In the 1870s and '80s the U.S. government adopted a policy of turning over the task of educating and "civilizing" Indians to the churches, and various Christian denominations were assigned to specific reservations. The practice was discontinued in the 1890s but not before the influence of some twenty-seven Christian sects became established among a number of tribes, particularly those whose native culture was in a state of disintegration.

About this same time the Bureau of Indian Affairs made a number of attempts to suppress native religion with a series of departmental regulations. It is ironic that the very people who took inordinate pride in the fact that their immigrant ancestors came to this country to escape religious persecution tolerated such a move. Begun as a frightened reaction to the Ghost Dance movement of the 1880s, the regulations were also directed against the Sun Dance of the Plains tribes and the rising strength of the Native American Church. This anti-Indian movement culminated in 1889 with a set of regulations known as the

When the Roll is Called Up Yonder

Yaaká'yú daako'doojíígo

Yaaká'yú daako'doojíígo

Yaaká'yú daako'doojíígo

Daako'doojíígee shíí itah dooleł.

From Apache Reader

Code of Religious Offenses. It was used as late as the 1920s in an attempt to crush Pueblo religion, restricting the times of the year and days of the week for native religious observances. It even restricted the number of participants and set age limits—all in an attempt to deny younger Indians the opportunity to participate and learn.

In a specific campaign against Taos, the religious leaders were accused of being "half animal" in their practice of "sadistic" and "obscene" *pagan* religion. And if that wasn't enough to swing public opinion against them, one U.S. senator also declared them and their friends to be un-American and agents of Moscow! (Situations or people don't seem to change very much.)

It was not until 1934 that this policy was reversed. Under John Collier's administration as Commissioner of Indian Affairs the following directive was issued: "No interference with Indian religious life or ceremonial expression will hereafter be tolerated. The cultural liberty of Indians is in all respects to be considered equal to that of any non-Indian group." Freedom of religion, the goal of so many white immigrants, was finally extended to America's original inhabitants.

The impact of Christianity upon Southwestern Indian religions is difficult to summarize except in broad generalizations. A minority accepted the new religion to the complete abandonment of native practices. A majority merely accommodated the new doctrines by modifying them to fit with native beliefs (losing nothing of the old while adding the new); this was primarily the case with the Rio Grande Pueblos. The Yaquis modified Catholicism into a form that suited their own needs but was not recognized by the Roman Catholic Church. Others, such as the followers of the Native American Church (the Peyote Cult) combined native and Christian beliefs to form an entirely new religious movement. And, of course, a surprising number, notably among the Hopi and Zuni, practice their native religion to the total exclusion of Christian beliefs.

Hopi and Papago plaques

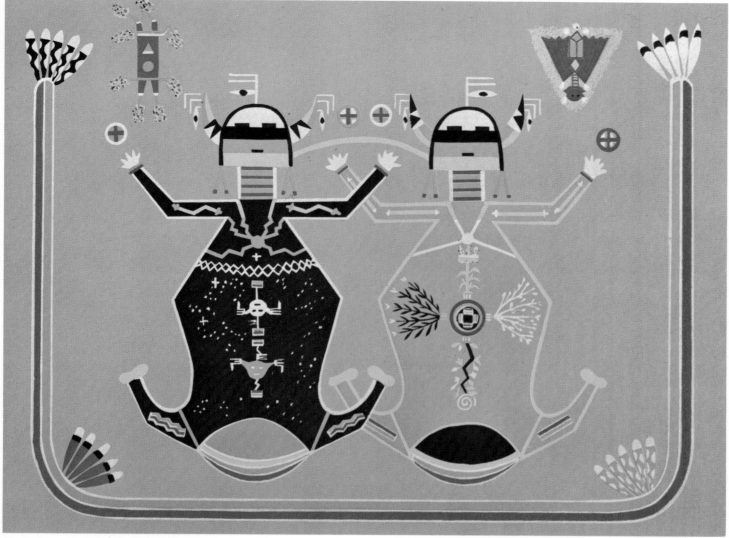

Sky Father, Earth Mother sandpainting

Navajo

THE EMERGENCE MYTH

In the beginning there was First Man, a deity transformed from an ear of corn. It was he who created the Universe.

The world today, by Navajo reckoning, is the fifth to be inhabited by the First People (other estimates vary from four to sixteen.) The four previous ones were located underground, each one a different color but none of them containing light. The First People lived in each of these worlds successively until they finally ascended to this one by making their way through a hollow reed. The actual Place-of-Emergence or Center-of-the-Universe is believed to be a badger hole in the mountains of southeastern Colorado.

At first the land was covered with water, a wet and disagreeable place, but in time the Holy People (another name for First People) transformed the earth into a liveable place and defined the boundaries of Navajoland. Mount Taylor in

New Mexico is the Southern or Turquoise Mountain; Mount Humphrey in the San Francisco Peaks near Flagstaff is the Western or Abalone Mountain. There is a difference of opinion over the exact identification of the Northern (Jet) and Eastern (White Shell) mountains. Light was created by First Man and First Woman who fashioned the moon, sun and stars of precious stones. An orderly arrangement planned for the stars was upset when Coyote, the ever present trickster, scattered them about the sky.

Evil also existed in the world in the form of monsters who had emerged from the underworlds and now they began to kill many of the Earth People. At this time a cradleboard containing a baby girl clothed in light magically appeared. She grew to become Ever-Changing Woman, sometimes identified as Earth with its constantly changing seasons or merely as Nature. Changing Woman eventually married Sun and Water and gave birth to twin boys, Monster Slayer and Born-of-Water. (In some versions of the story Changing Woman—or Turquoise

Woman—and her sister, White Shell Woman, married, respectively, Sun and Water and gave birth to the Twin War Gods.)

The exploits of the Twin War Gods form a goodly part of Navajo mythology. In their journeys they encountered and succeeded in slaying many of the monsters which were bothering the Earth People. They failed only in dispatching Old Age, Poverty, Sickness and Death. Throughout Navajo country is evidence of the Twins' battles. A lava flow east of Grants, New Mexico is the dried blood of a slain monster. Shiprock is the remains of a man-eating eagle and various volcanic peaks are the heads of monsters decapitated by the War Gods.

It was Changing Woman who finally created human beings, using flakes of skin from her own body. She formed six groups of people, believed by some to represent the first Navajo clans.

There is no supreme being in Navajo religion. The most powerful and most important deities include Changing Woman, Sun, and the Twin War Gods. Of these only Changing Woman is consistently helpful to man. Changing Woman lives on an island in the Western Sea where she is visited daily by her husband, Sun. All other deities are capable of both good and evil and are sometimes classified on the basis of how difficult they are to persuade to be helpful.

Lesser deities include *Yeis*—the male and female figures that are depicted in sandpaintings and represent such forces found in nature as wind, thunder and lightning. Still less important among the list of Holy People are the ancestors of animals and plants and figures identified with specific geographical locations.

AFTERWORLD

The Anglo concept of an Indian's "Happy Hunting Ground" does not apply to the Navajo (nor to many Indian tribes, for that matter). *This* is the life that is important and it is not considered as a mere preparation for another world. Neither is there a concept of another world for eternal punishment. The Afterworld is shadowy and ill-defined, a dull but not unpleasant place, underground "to the north" which is reached by four days' travel after death.

Death is considered inevitable and therefore not so much feared as the dead themselves. Since the deceased are always the possible source of *chindi* or malevolent ghosts they are disposed of as quickly as possible and with strict performance of all required rituals. Any error may offend the deceased and cause the *chindi* to seek revenge.

CURING CEREMONIES

The Navajo concept of the universe in an ideal state is one in which all parts—each with its power for good and evil—are maintained in interrelated harmony. The balance, at best, is precarious and may be upset intentionally by ghosts or witches or unintentionally by persons who break a religious taboo or unwittingly come in contact with snakes, bears or lightning. To cross the path of a bear or touch a piece of wood that came from a lightning-struck tree is enough to upset the balance.

Sacrificial figurines are sometimes used to correct the damage done by the violation of minor taboos. An unborn child may be injured if the mother sees blood or a wounded animal during her pregnancy. To prevent injury or sickness to the child a medicine man performs a brief ceremony during which he carves a figure from wood and places it near an ancient ruin, a location of easy access to the supernaturals.

Navajo singer directs the making of a sandpainting. Andy Tsinajinnie

Illness, physical and mental, is the result of upsetting the harmony. Conversely the cure for illness is to restore the patient to harmony. It is to this end—the preservation or restoration of harmony—that Navajo religious ceremonies are performed.

To determine the cause of a particular illness is the job of a diagnostician—*ndilniihii* or "hand trembler." Prayer, concentration and the application of sacred pollen to the patient causes the priest-practitioner's hand to tremble; it is from these movements that the exact cause of the illness is determined.

The cause of the sickness determines the ceremony or "sing" needed to effect a cure. Also called "chants" or "ways," these sings are based on Navajo mythology. They consist of complicated ceremonies lasting from one to nine nights and include the use of chants, songs, prayers, dances, prayer sticks, herbs, emetics, sweat baths and sandpaintings, all performed under the direction of a "singer" or priest-practitioner, known in Navajo as a *hatathli*.

There are six main groups of chants or song ceremonials although some have become obsolete through disuse. The Blessingway rites are not curing rites but are performed for general well-being, to ensure, as the Navajos put it, that one may "walk in beauty."

The curing ceremonials or chantways are concerned with specific illnesses. The Bead Chant cures skin diseases. The Shooting Chant is used against disease attributable to lightning or snakes. Insanity and paralysis require the Night Chant while nervousness can be alleviated with Mountain Way. The Windways cures disease caused by evil winds and covers a host of afflictions ranging from poor vision, insomnia and hoarseness to tuberculosis, heart trouble, snakebite, and even alcoholism.

There are probably over fifty chants or "ways," not counting the variations. Most singers or priest-practitioners know two or three complete chants and specialize in those. It would be impossible for one man to know all of the complicated rituals for over a dozen curing rites.

The performance of a lengthy curing rite is an expensive affair and taxes the finances of the patient's entire extended family. Not only is the *hatathli* well paid, but tremendous quantities of food must be provided for guests—and they arrive from far and wide to share the blessings derived from attending the ceremonies and to take part in the related social activities.

The patient, through the rituals, becomes purified and eventually identified with the deities whose help is sought. From them he obtains power and overcomes the evil causing the illness, thereby restoring him to harmony with the universe. Once again he "walks in beauty." The sense of security and well-being the patient derives from the host of friends and fellow tribesmen who surround him during the ceremony is also conducive to his recovery.

SANDPAINTINGS

Sandpaintings, probably the best known portion of the lengthy curing rites, are used by most tribes in the Southwest. The Navajos, however, have developed them to the greatest degree and recognize between 600 and 1000 separate designs.

Drypaintings, as they are sometimes called,

The contents of a singer's medicine bundle will vary depending on the "chant" or "way" for which it is intended but all items are identified with some incident in Navajo mythology. For example, the otter fur collar with the reed whistle attached relates to an episode in which the otter loaned its skin to the Twin War Gods when the Sun attempted to freeze them. The crystals in the miniature basket are symbolic of light, fire, and truth and are used ceremonially to light prayer sticks. In many legends they provide both illumination and fire.

To the left of the collar is a feathered male asperger with which liquid medicines are sprinkled on both patient and sandpainting. The wide painted boards (tsintel), made from the wood of a lightning-struck cottonwood tree, bear pictures of Father Sky, Mother Earth, and Lightning. The four crooked snakes, each representing a cardinal direction, are related to lightning.

In the center of the picture, leaning against an agave fireboard, is a male bullroarer (tsin-di-nih). Made of oak and set with turquoise, it reproduces the sound of thunder when whirled and drives away evil.

Medicine bundles are often depicted in sandpaintings. A pair of them usually guard the eastern entrance to the painting, the only side not protected by the rainbow.

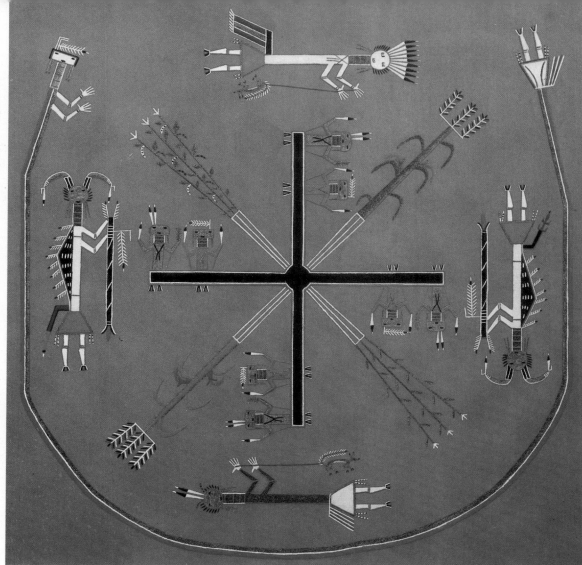

Whirling Logs sandpainting, the theme of the Night and Feather Chants. In the center are depicted the four sacred plants of the Navajos: corn, squash, beans and tobacco.

Navajo singer completes a Whirling Logs sandpainting. Later the patient will be seated on the painting and portions of it which relate to the illness will be placed on the patient's body. Later the painting will be ceremonially destroyed and buried in order to dispose of the evil it absorbed during the rite.
Clifford Beck

Talking God, carrying a sacred fawn skin, leads the Yeibichai Dancers. Johnny Secatero

use pulverized minerals and charcoal to form the patterns although vegetal material such as pollen and corn meal may also be used. They range in size from one to twenty feet in diameter and may require a dozen or more persons working most of a day to complete. The sandpainting is created and destroyed between sunrise and sunset of one day.

The sandpainting is a symbolic representation of some portion of Navajo mythology. The patient is seated on the sandpainting after it is completed and parts of it are placed on his body. By identifying in this way with the deities invoked, he gains power from them. The evil which has caused the sickness is absorbed by the sand and is then ceremonially buried.

The colors used in drypaintings are usually symbolic of direction; as a general rule white is east, yellow is west, black (a male color) is north and blue (female) is south; red represents sunshine.

YEIBICHAI DANCE

The Night Chant or Night Way—more commonly referred to as the *Yeibichai*—is a major winter curing ceremony that can be held only after the snakes are asleep and there is no longer danger of lightning. The rite is performed to cure patients of nervousness or insanity. It is a dangerous ritual, for mistakes made by either the patient or singer during its performance can result in crippling, facial paralysis or a loss of sight or hearing.

The name *Yeibichai* is used for the Night Way because of the appearance of numerous *Yeis* (masked representations of supernatural beings which possess great powers) during the last two nights of this nine-day ceremony.

On the eighth night the *Yebichais* conduct an initiation rite to introduce young Navajo boys and girls to the secret of the masked gods. The children first have their hair washed—a standard act of purification among most Southwestern tribes—and then white clay is daubed on their bodies.

The boys are blessed with sacred meal and then ceremonially whipped with yucca leaves by the masked figures. The girls are marked on the feet, hands, shoulders and head with corn meal and touched with ears of white and yellow corn wrapped in spruce twigs.

Shortly afterwards the *Yeis* remove their masks so the children learn they are really ordinary human beings who only play the part of supernatural figures. *Hastseyalti*, the Talking God of the East, places his mask on each of the boys while *Hasttse-baad*, the female *Yei*, places hers on the girls so that each child may view the world through the eyes of the *Yeibichais*.

Adults often take part in this ritual for it is necessary for each Navajo to participate in the

Yei masks are made of buckskin from deer which have been ceremonially killed. The spilling of blood must be avoided, so the death of the animal is caused by suffocation with sacred meal or pollen.

Top two masks are those of the Twin War Gods, Born-of-Water (the hourglass figures represent scalps) and Monster Slayer. The horned mask is that of the Humpbacked God. Black God's mask bears symbols of a crescent moon and the Pleiades (white dots at upper left).

Navajo yei figures collect food and pollen during the Night Chant. Tom Woodard collection

Ceremonial staff carrier for the Enemy Way or Squaw Dance ceremony. Harrison Begay

Navajo Fire Dancers. Andy Tsinajinnie

initiation ceremony four times during his lifetime.

Throughout the ninth night *Yeibichai* dance teams perform, each group singing in the falsetto voice for which these dancers are noted.

SQUAW DANCE

The *Entah* or Enemy Way—commonly referred to as a Squaw Dance by non-Navajos—is a war ceremonial conducted only during the summer months. Formerly it was given as a purification rite for warriors who had been contaminated by contact with the enemy. Now it may be performed for persons whose sickness has been diagnosed as resulting from contact with whites or other non-Navajos.

The *Entah* is a three-day ritual which begins at the patient's hogan and moves to a new location on each succeeding day—usually a day's ride away by horseback. Much of the time between specific parts of the rite is spent in racing, gambling and listening to informal talks by recognized leaders.

Yeibichai figures carved by Clitso,
noted Navajo medicine man from Chinle

A spectator gets a dunking by the Black Dancers during the Mud ceremonial. Clifford Bec

On the third day the Black Dancers—the clowns of the War Ceremony—perform a Mud "Dance". Emerging from the smoke hole of the hogan they seize the patient and toss him into the air. Afterwards they stretch him face down in a mudhole while they attempt to loosen the hold of evil spirits which are causing the sickness by running over the patient. After this ritual is completed, spectators are fair game and those caught are also given a mud bath.

The Squaw Dance is performed on the third night and is primarily a "coming out" event for eligible young females. The girls, with much encouragement from their mothers, invite young men to join them in a round dance. At the end of several rounds the man is required to make a token payment to the girl for the privilege of dancing with her. The squaw dance is an all night affair performed to the accompaniment of a chorus and drummer.

Fire Dance

The Mountain Chant or Mountain Top Way is a winter ceremonial; to be given when there is still the possibility that summer thunderstorms or spring windstorms might cause death by snakebite or lightning. The Mountain Chant gets its name from the dwelling place of the deities

whose aid is invoked during the ceremony. The names Fire Dance or Corral Dance are derived from rituals performed as part of the nine-day ceremonial.

On the ninth night of the chant, a huge semicircular corral of evergreen is erected. It is here that medicine men perform magical feats: a yucca plant appears to grow and blossom in a matter of minutes; men swallow arrows; a feather dances unaided, or a sun symbol may climb out of a basket and up a pole and then return to its container.

Afterwards the Fire Dancers appear, daubed with white clay, and carrying torches of cedar bark which they light at the huge central fire. They dash in and out of the fire with impunity, lashing themselves and their fellow dancers with flaming torches. This is a purification ritual which completes the Mountain Chant. After the Fire Dance, spectators pick up bits of the charred cedar bark as a charm against fire.

Rio Grande pueblo woman's dance *tablita* with cloud motifs

Rio Grande Pueblos

Keresan Emergence Myth

The emergence myth varies somewhat in detail among the seven Keresan-speaking pueblos. The version given here relies primarily on Santa Ana and Santo Domingo accounts.

In the beginning the people lived in the innermost of the Underworlds. Seeking light they moved progressively upward through four worlds, each of a different color, white, red, blue and yellow.

With the aid of various plants, animals and birds an attempt was made to break through the crust of the present world. Finally a badger, standing on an eagle's nest built on top of a spruce tree succeeded in enlarging a hole made by a woodpecker until it was big enough to allow people to pass through.

Assisted by *Iatik*, Mother of All, they emerged at *Shipap*, the Center of the World. The world was still wet and soft until the Sun, father of the Twin War Gods, dried it and made it habitable.

Shipap was too sacred a place in which to dwell so the people left to seek another location. Only *Iatik* remained, but before the people left she gave them her heart—corn—and instructed the *caciques* (religious leaders) to care for the people as she had done. She also told the people to return to *Shipap* at death.

The people wandered about and finally settled at White House (an unidentified site "to the north" of their present villages). Here they dwelt with the deities who taught them all that was necessary for their life in this world. The *katsinas* appeared among them to dance for rain and the *Koshare* and *Kwirena* came to help make the crops grow.

Although life was good at White House, eventually groups began to leave to seek new places; each became a new tribe in doing so. The Keresans also left and moved southward until they reached their present locations. No longer do the masked gods live among the people and now it is necessary for the people themselves to impersonate the deities and perform the dances to ensure the well-being of the pueblos.

The Creation and Cosmos

Thought Woman, the deity who created all things by thinking them into existence, is responsible for the world as it appears. She may also be the same figure as Spider Grandmother, another deity to whom the same role is attributed.

The Keresans envisage the earth as the center of the universe with all other planets functioning in order to make the earth liveable. The Sun is referred to as "Father" and is an important deity. The Sky is "in charge" of the earth and its people. The earth itself is referred to as "Mother." Maize is also called "Mother."

Afterworld

At birth each person receives a soul and a guardian spirit from *Iariko* (or *Iatik*), the Mother of All. At the time of death both the soul and guardian leave the body but remain in the house of the deceased for four days before making the journey to *Shipap*, the entrance to the Underworld. The guardian spirit carries a prayer stick, necessary for the admission of the soul to *Shipap*. Depending on the virtue of the individual, the soul is assigned to one of the four Underworlds. Those qualified to enter the innermost world become *Shiwana* (rainmakers) and return to the villages in the form of clouds.

Death is explained as a natural and necessary phenomenon for "if nobody died there would soon be no room left in the world."

Blue Corn Maiden. Gilbert Atencio

Zia clown. Rafael Medina

CORN DANCE

Corn has always been the basis of Pueblo life. To maintain the precarious balance of an agricultural economy in this land of little rain requires the cooperation of all forces, natural and supernatural. It is not surprising, therefore, that all religious ceremonies (except for curing rites) revolve around the cultivation and propagation of corn.

Constant references to Earth Mother and Corn Mother indicate that agriculture is more than just a practical art but goes far beyond to encompass the philosophy and religion of the Pueblo Indians.

The Corn Dance, commonly performed during the spring and summer months, may be given at any time. Although its purpose is always the propagation of corn, it may be performed to mark the annual installation of new secular officers of the pueblo, or the village's Catholic saint's day.

The dance, as with all Southwestern ceremonies, is a combination of song, drama, dance and poetry which forms a prayer for rain, bountiful harvests, the propagation of animals and plants, and the well-being of the pueblo and all those who attend.

All Rio Grande Pueblos perform the Corn Dance. Perhaps the largest and most impressive is given at the village of Santo Domingo on the fourth of August—Saint Dominic's Day—the village's saint.

Early in the morning of the fourth, the Indians attend mass at the church just outside of the pueblo. On this day, baptisms and marriages are performed and recorded for the previous year. The statue of Saint Dominic is removed from the church, paraded through the village streets to the beating of a snare drum and the firing of guns, and then deposited in a temporary shelter of cottonwood branches in the dance plaza. The saint is guarded by the pueblo's officers and the noise of guns and snare drum continues while the dancers pay homage to Saint Dominic. After this the day is devoted to the native ceremonial. Catholicism and Pueblo religion exist side by side, but there is no real mixing of the two.

The pueblo's population is divided into two halves or moieties; the Squash, or Winter People, and the Turquoise, or Summer People. Each division is responsible for village affairs during six months of the year. The dancers of each moiety perform alternately during the day.

Each kiva, the Squash and Turquoise, provides its own *Koshares*, chorus, drummer, standard bearer and corn dancers—usually numbering well over 200 persons. The bodies of the male Squash moiety dancers are painted with a yellow

Sun symbol bearer of the Green Corn Dance. Tonita Pena

Corn Mother fetishes. Roger Tsabetsaye

ochre, those of the Turquoise group with a blue-grey clay.

The first figures to appear are the *Koshares* of the Turquoise moiety, their bodies painted horizontally in black and white stripes and dressed in ragged black breechcloths. On their wrists and moccasins are worn strips of rabbit fur; their hair is tied up in "horns" decorated with cornhusks. The *Kurena* of the Squash kiva are similarly attired except their bodies are divided vertically, one half painted white with black spots and the other half yellow ochre. Both wear deer hoof rattles at the waist.

As invisible spirits of the deceased, the *Koshare* and *Kurena* possess much power to bring rain clouds, and to influence the growth of crops. Related to the Sun, their home is in the east. During the dance they magically protect the pueblo and its inhabitants from all enemies. They also perform many practical services for the dancers by making needed adjustments or repairs to dancers' costumes during the performances.

As clowns they pantomime, with exaggerated gestures, the chorus or the dancers themselves. Between dances they indulge in ribald horseplay, much to the delight of the spectators and the chagrin of their victims.

Rio Grande Pueblo Buffalo Dance. Tonita Pena

The chorus, made up of fifty or more men, and the drummer are next to appear. They are dressed in loose fitting bright colored shirts and trousers split at the ankle. Each carries sprigs of evergreen—a symbol of growing things and everlasting life. Although the chants follow a traditional rhythmic form they are often composed anew each year. The expressive movements of the chorus mimic the words which describe the gathering of the clouds from the four directions, the falling rain and the growing plants.

The main procession of corn dancers is led by a man who bears the sun symbol; this consists of a long pole (representing the fir tree which enabled the people to climb up from the underworld) from which is suspended a dance kilt decorated with eagle feathers and a fox pelt. Fastened to the end of the pole is a painted gourd (containing sacred seeds) and a dazzling cluster of macaw feathers. Under this banner the dancers perform. The weaving of the sun symbol over the corn dancers constitutes both a blessing and a purification and a request to the *Shiwana*—the rain cloud people—to bless the pueblo with moisture.

The male corn dancers are dressed in white cotton kilts embroidered with symbols of clouds and rain (this was formerly the ordinary attire of the Pueblo men). Over this is tied the white, tasselled rain sash. From the back of the belt is suspended a fox skin; a reminder of man's common ancestry with the animals, when all had tails. Behind the right knee is tied a turtle shell rattle with deer hoof tinklers. In the right hand is a gourd rattle with which the sound of falling rain is imitated. Skunk fur worn over the moccasins protects the wearer from evil. A bandoleer hung over the left shoulder is decorated with *conus* shells from the Pacific ocean. A cluster of parrot feathers is worn on top of the head; the plumage of this bird is believed to bring rain from the south. Personal jewelry and sprigs of evergreen complete the costume.

The female dancers wear the black *manta* tied at the waist with a red and green belt. In most pueblos they are barefoot. In each hand they carry evergreen boughs. Their hair hangs loose in imitation of the long wisps of summer rain that sweep the land. On their heads are worn *tablitas*, thin wooden boards cut in a terraced cloud pattern and either pierced or painted with sun or star designs.

It is customary for the casual observer to label Indian dances and the accompanying music "monotonous." It may appear that way if one does not know the language, of course, but even a slightly alert visitor will soon recognize the complicated rhythms and dance steps that are employed and anyone who attempts to "keep the beat" will find himself confused by the frequent unexpected changes.

The moieties dance alternately during the day; both groups and their choruses combine for a spectacular final performance at the end of the day.

San Ildefonso Deer Dancer. Tse Ye Mu

HUNTING CEREMONIALS

Hunting was formerly an important activity. Deer were the most common game animals but antelope, elk, and mountain sheep were also hunted for meat and hides. The Rio Grande pueblo people ventured onto the Great Plains occasionally to hunt buffalo, a dangerous journey that exposed them to attack from hostile tribes which jealously guarded their territories against trespassers.

To be successful in hunting a man had to have more than just practical skills; he also needed the cooperation of the animals he hunted and it was to this end that most hunting rituals were directed. This was not a matter of a superior

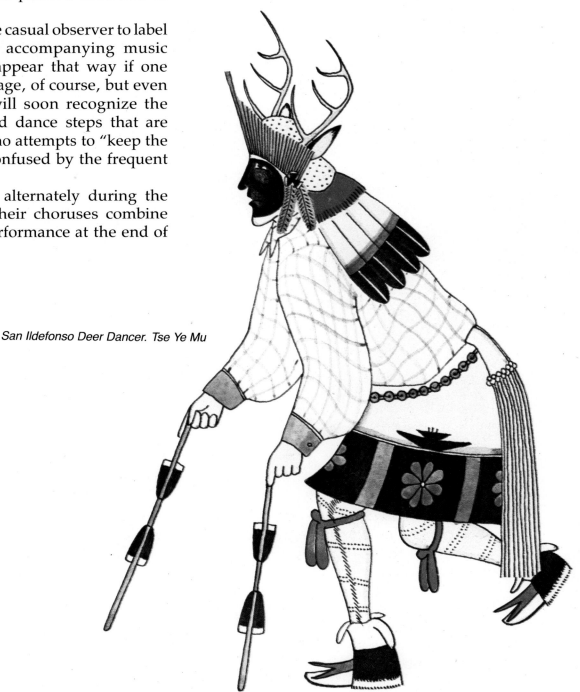

being attempting to control a lower life form but one in which two equals sought an understanding of their respective roles in the scheme of life. As the cloven-hoofed mammals must eat plants to survive, so must man rely on the animals, in turn, to sustain himself.

The hunting dances not only honored the animals but also ensured their propagation; further, they gained the cooperation and permission of the game so that the hunters could take those that were needed for food and clothing.

Even today hunting requires many separate rites before, during and after the hunt. Fetishes are used in an effort to obtain assistance from the beasts of prey, the expert hunters of the animal world. If a hunter is successful, he first removes the heart from the game and "feeds" it to his fetish. Tobacco, corn meal and a prayer feather may be offered to the dead animal to appease its spirit.

Upon returning to the village the game "lies in state" in the home of the hunter, wrapped in a

Jemez Pueblo
deer dancer's headdress

Buffalo and Antelope Dancers. The power of the buffalo is often sought to cure the sick. A buffalo headdress, touched to a patient after a dance, is believed to have curative powers. Rafael Medina

Tesuque Eagle Dancer. Paul Vigil

ceremonial robe and greeted as a visitor by those who enter the house. Anything less than this ritual treatment would offend the animals and the deity who is in charge of all game.

Respect for the animal continues even after it has been consumed. The skulls of deer and elk are painted with clay, and prayer feathers are hung from the antlers before being placed on the housetop. During the animal dances the homes bearing skulls are visited by the dancers. The bones of these animals are never thrown to the dogs but are blessed with corn meal and ceremonially deposited in the Rio Grande.

Animal Dances

Animal dances in the Rio Grande pueblos are usually winter ceremonials. The number of participants varies greatly and may include as few as a pair of Buffalo dancers and a Buffalo Woman, who represents the Mother of All Game, or a massed group of deer, elk, buffalo, antelope and mountain sheep impersonators plus a hunt chief, hunters, drummer and chorus.

Hopi Eagle Kachina with the moisture tablet or shield visible on its back

Hoop Dancer. Guy Nez Jr.

A typical Tewa animal ceremonial begins the night preceding the dance. Small fires are built in the plaza and on the housetops to guide the animals to the village. At dawn the Hunt Chief calls in the animals from the surrounding hills and leads them along paths of sacred meal into the plaza where they dance. The impersonators often carry two sticks with which they imitate the movements of the forefeet of the animals.

In Keresan pueblos a young female performer races into the hills in the early morning where she "captures" the animal dancers and leads them to the village. The dance plaza is planted with small evergreens and in this artificial forest the animal impersonators dance. At the end of the performance "hunters" shoot the dancers with arrows of straw and carry them off to their houses where they are honored as slain game. This ritual assures the hunter's success when he goes out after real game.

EAGLE DANCE

The eagle plays an important role in Pueblo mythology. A powerful bird, it often soars out of sight so that it is believed to maintain a close relationship with the Sun. Its power is often sought

Koshare *is the Keresan name for this figure; its Tewa name is* Kossa. *At Taos it is called* Chiffonete, *a term reportedly of "border Spanish" origin.*
Gilbert Atencio

in curing rites and its plumage is an essential part of many costumes of both masked and unmasked dancers. The fluff feathers represent the "breath of life" and are used as prayer plumes by all tribes.

A favorite performance at public exhibitions, the Eagle Dance is also given in the villages. The ritual, performed by young men who imitate the eagles' flight, depicts man's affinity with the sky deities through the eagle as intermediary. The dancers often wear a decorated shield on their backs. To some this indicates the eagle is the chief of birds; others refer to the shield as a "moisture tablet," an acknowledgment of the eagle's ability to bring rain.

Hoop Dance

The origin of the Hoop Dance is unknown but there is some suggestion that it was originally a symbolic reenactment of man's emergence from the Underworld. Today it is staged at most public exhibitions as a spectacular acrobatic performance. The dancers are usually dressed in costumes of the Plains Indian variety.

Replica of a Zuni War God

Zuni

The Zuni have probably the most complex of all native religions in the Southwest, and every aspect of Zuni life is completely integrated with their religion. Numerous religious organizations, through an intricate system of interlocking ceremonials, interrelate the whole of Zuni culture.

Six esoteric cults (in addition to the ancestor cult to which all Zuni belong), form the basis of Zuni ceremonialism. These are the cults of the Sun, Rainmakers (this cult is in charge of twelve priesthoods), *Koko* (or kachinas), Priests of the *Koko*, War Gods, and Beast Gods (representing the animal patrons of twelve related curing societies). Each cult has its own priests, fetishes, rituals and ceremonial calendar.

Basic to the religious philosophy of the Zuni is the recognition of man's oneness with the universe and the absolute necessity of maintaining this harmony through the correct execution of prescribed rituals. If the ceremonies are properly performed, the rains will fall, harvests will be bountiful, the life of the people will be long and happy, and the fertility of the plant and animal worlds will continue.

CREATION MYTH

In the beginning there was only fog and mists; "above" existed three deities, *Awonawilona*—a bisexual supreme being (the Creator of All), Sun, the giver of light, warmth and life, and Moon, the deity responsible for dividing the year into twelve months and delineating the life span of man. "Below" existed two superhuman beings, *Shiwanni* and his wife *Shiwanokia*.

Awonawilona created clouds and water with the breath of his heart. *Shiwanni* formed the constellations from bubbles of his saliva. *Shiwanokia*, using her saliva, created Mother Earth. The *Ashiwi* (Zuni) are the children of *Shiwanni* and *Shiwanokia*; they were born in the innermost of the underworlds.

EMERGENCE AND MIGRATION MYTH

The underworld which the *Ashiwi* inhabited was totally dark; the people lived in holes and subsisted on wild grass seeds. They are said to have been peculiar creatures with tails, gigantic ears, webbed hands and feet, moss-covered bodies and a foul odor.

Sun Father created two sons, *Kowwituma* and *Watsusi*, out of bits of foam and sent them to the Underworld to bring the *Ashiwi* into the upperworld. The sons, known as the Divine Ones, made light for the people by kindling fire. Following a path marked with sacred meal they led the *Ashiwi* to the North where they planted a Ponderosa pine. They climbed the tree to make their way into the third or Water Moss World. The next trail led to the West; here a Douglas fir was grown to allow the *Ashiwi* to enter the second or Mud World. The third trail went South to an aspen which was used to reach the first or World of Wings (sun's rays). The last journey was to the East and the people climbed a silver spruce to emerge into upperworld. The actual entry was made through a spring or lake whose waters parted to allow the passage of the *Ashiwi*.

At the time of emergence the Divine Ones used their stone knives to transform the animal-like *Ashiwi* into human form. They also taught the Zuni how to make fire and to cook their food. Corn was acquired from two witches who managed to escape from the Underworld at the time of emergence.

The Zuni then began their wanderings to seek the Middle Place (the middle of the world) where they were to settle. Many years were spent in the search and numerous villages were built only to be later abandoned.

At one stage in the wanderings the *Shiwanni* of the North sent his son and daughter to seek a village site. During their search the brother suddenly became enamored of his sister's beauty and possessed her. The same night ten offspring were born to them; the first was normal and became the ancestor of the *Korkoskshi*, the rain makers. The other nine became the *Koyemshi* (Mudheads), the idiot hybrids of this incestuous union.

The brother created the Zuni and Little Colorado rivers, by marking the sands with his foot, and at their junction a lake (Listening Spring) was formed. Within the waters of the lake he created a village, *Kothluwalawa* (sometimes called *Wenima*), the home of the Council of Gods.

The Council of Gods came into being as the result of a river crossing by the *Ashiwi* during

Zuni fetish jar and bowl. Fetishes are stored in the large jar and "fed" through the hole in the side.

Shalako participants: Yamuhakto, Sholawitsi, Hututu, Shalako and alternate, Sayatasha, Yamuhakto and Salimopya. Ray Naha

their migration. The children of the Wood Fraternity were being carried through the stream but became panicky and fell into the water. Immediately they were transformed into various water creatures—turtles, tadpoles, frogs and snakes—which made their way to *Kothluwalawa*. Here they matured instantly and became the Council of the Gods.

In their migration to the Middle Place the *Ashiwi* were stopped by a tribe known as *Kianakwe* which was led by *Chakwena*, the Keeper of Game. The Divine Ones grew weary of leading the *Ashiwi* in fighting the *Kianakwe* so petitioned their Sun Father to send them two War Gods as replacements. The Sun impregnated a waterfall and the *Ahayuta* (as the War Gods are known in time of peace) or *Uyuyewi* and *Masailema* (as they were known in time of war) were created.

With the help of the War Gods the *Ashiwi* defeated the *Kianakwe* in a four-day battle. They captured their village and released the wild game held captive by *Chakwena*. The ruins of this village are said to be some fifty miles south of the present town of Zuni.

The Zuni continued to wander and lived in several villages (the ruins of which may still be seen) before they finally located the Middle Place, *Itiwanna*, the native name for Zuni pueblo.

AFTERWORLD

At death the corpse is bathed in yucca suds and rubbed with corn meal before burial. The spirit of the dead lingers in the village for four days during which time the door of its former home is left ajar to permit its entry. On the morning of the fifth day the spirit goes to the Council of Gods in the village of *Kothluwalawa* beneath the water of Listening Spring. Here the spirit becomes a rainmaker—a member of the *Uwannami*. If the deceased is a member of the Bow Priesthood, he becomes a lightning maker who brings water from the "six great waters of the world." The water, in the form of rain, is poured through the clouds which are believed to be masks worn by the *Uwannami*.

SHALAKO

The *Shalako*, a winter ceremony held in late November or early December, is the major ritual performed at the pueblo of Zuni. Usually referred to as a house blessing ceremonial, it is a forty-nine day reenactment of the Zuni emergence and migration myths. In addition it is a prayer for rain, for the health and well being of the people, and for the propagation of plants and animals. During the *Shalako* the spirits of the dead return to be honored and fed. During the final hour of this

Salimopya

Shalako

Salimopya

Sholawitsi

Zuni kachina dolls can usually be distinguished from Hopi dolls by their long, attenuated form and movable arms. Cloth and leather are commonly added to provide costume details. Pine is often used instead of cottonwood.

lengthy ceremonial a hunting rite is also performed. The description that follows can do little more than touch the surface of this highly complex ceremonial.

Participants in the *Shalako* (impersonators and the sponsors of the *Shalako* houses) are chosen during the previous winter solstice ceremony. Preparations for the numerous and varied rites begin immediately afterward and occupy much of the participants' time for the intervening ten months. Long and complicated chants must be learned, prayer sticks must be placed each month at certain shrines which mark the migrations of the Zuni in ancient times, and minor rituals must be performed *each month*.

In addition to this the houses which will honor the *Shalakos* must be built or extensively re-modelled. Ideally eight houses are used, six for the *Shalakos*, one for *Sayatasha* and the Council of Gods (usually called the Long Horn House) and one for the *Koyemshi*. Occasionally, however, it is necessary to double up the *Shalakos* when not enough houses are available. To sponsor a *Shalako* house is a tremendously expensive undertaking; added to the actual cost of construction is the expense of providing food for the participants and a myriad of visitors.

The principal masked figures which appear during the ceremony are:

Shalakos—the Giant Couriers of the Rainmakers—one to represent each of the six kivas. The masks of these ten-foot figures are carried on poles by the impersonators. Each *Shalako* has two impersonators who take turns dancing.

Sayatasha—the Rain God of the North—often called the Long Horn for the projection of the right side of his mask which symbolizes long life for the people. *Sayatasha* oversees all the activities preceding the actual appearance of the *Shalakos*.

Hututu—the Rain God of the South—is the deputy of *Sayatasha*. Both carry rattles of deer scapulae, bows and arrows, and numerous prayer plumes.

Sholawitsi—the Fire God—is a representative of the Sun. The part is always played by a young boy from the Badger Clan. *Sholawitsi* carries a fawn skin filled with seeds.

Model of a Zuni shrine with masks of two Salimopya *and* Sholawitsi

Planting the prayersticks and blessing the shrines. Mac Schweitzer

Yamuhakto—these two figures have sticks of cottonwood tied to the tops of their masks which represent their authority over forests and trees. The antlers they carry are symbolic of the deer which live in the forests. The Yamuhakto are also called Warriors of the West and East.

Salimopya—are the warriors who carry yucca whips to guard the performers and keep the spectators from coming too close. They may come from any of the six kivas but only two appear during the Shalako.

Koyemshi—the Mudheads—are led by Awan Tachu, Great Father. The others are called Deputy to the Great Father, Warrior, Bat, Small Horns, Old Grandfather, Old Youth, Water Drinker, Game Maker and Small Mouth.

The Council of Gods is made up of Sayatasha, Hututu, two Yamuhakto, and Sholawitsi.

Eight days before the arrival of the Shalakos, the Koyemshi appear in the village to exhort the people to complete their preparations for the coming of the gods.

Four days later Sholawitsi and Sayatasha arrive from the west having retraced the migration of the Ashiwi. The Fire God lights fires on the way to guide the Council of Gods to the Middle Place.

First Day of the Shalako

Sholawitsi and Sayatasha appear in the village to inspect the six holes—one for each kiva—that have been dug to receive prayer plumes. Later in the day the Fire God and his ceremonial father deposit their prayer sticks. They are followed by Sayatasha, Hututu and two Yamuhakto who bless the shrines in brief ceremonies and also leave prayer plumes. They then retreat to their Shalako house to perform blessing ceremonies for the building, and the altar which has been installed, and to place special prayer sticks near the roof beams. After this they smoke cigarettes of native tobacco. The smoke, symbolic of clouds, will bring rain to the land.

At dark the giant Shalakos arrive at the south side of the river where they use a narrow footbridge to cross over into the village. Upon reaching the north side the impersonators leave their masks to go to their special houses. They return

Shalakos racing. Mac Schweitzer

shortly and the birdlike creatures approach the houses with much clacking of beaks and strange whistling sounds. Before they enter, the houses must be properly blessed in ceremonies similar to those conducted at the Long Horn house.

After bringing the *Shalako* inside, the impersonator leaves his mask and enters into a lengthy chant dialogue with the sponsor of the house. This recitation of the emergence and migration myth consumes a great part of the evening. Food is then taken by the *Shalako* impersonators to the river where it is offered to the spirits of the dead which live at *Kothluwalawa*.

General feasting follows and the kitchens of the *Shalako* houses turn out unbelievable quantities of food for performers, townspeople and visitors.

Dancing by the *Shalakos* begins after midnight. The *Salimopyas* and *Koyemshi* also make the rounds to all of the *Shalako* houses to perform. A Zuni version of the Navajo *Yeibichai* is also staged—to the great delight of the Navajos who are present. It is said this dance commemorates a time when the Navajos performed this ceremony

at Zuni to cure the people of an epidemic that caused swellings.

The dancing continues until sunrise at which time *Sayatasha* climbs to a rooftop to offer prayers on behalf of the Zuni people. The dancers are purified with a hair washing rite.

Second Day

About noon the following day (the forty-ninth) the *Shalakos* and their attendants leave the pueblo and cross the river to an open field south of the village. Here the *Shalakos* "race" to place prayer plumes in six excavations before returning to *Kothluwalawa*. The race depicts the manner in which the *Shalakos*, as couriers of the gods, deliver messages and prayers for rain throughout the year.

As the *Shalakos* disappear in the distance, the young men run to catch them. Those who succeed in capturing a *Shalako* believe they will have future success in hunting deer.

Old Zuni kachina dolls

Pautiwa

Anahoho

Kachinas approach a kiva for a night performance of the Corn Maiden marionettes. Ray Naha

Hopi Pueblos

EMERGENCE MYTH

Each Hopi village has its own particular version of the emergence myth, and legends which trace the wanderings of the Hopis before they reached their present location vary with each clan.

Huruing Wuuti (in some legends it is Spider Woman) is credited with creating mankind out of saliva and colored sand. Four sets of male and female figures, black, red, yellow and white, were made; each was given a different language and the power to reproduce. Life began in the innermost of four Underworlds. Some legends depict life there as good, with animals and people living in harmony and in the midst of plenty. Others maintain the underworlds were dark and overcrowded and the upward journey was an attempt to alleviate those unpleasant conditions.

Most of the stories allude to social disorder caused by Two-Hearts (evil persons). The dissension and fighting that followed caused the people to forget their ceremonies and life plan. In disgust *Sotuqnangu* (God of the Sky) destroyed, in turn, each underworld in an attempt to wipe out the Two-Hearts. Each time a few good people were saved to populate the new world only to repeat the mistakes of the previous one.

To escape the flood that was used to destroy the third Underworld and its people who had

sage of the people.

The One Horned priests stayed below to prevent the Two-Hearts from reaching the upperworld. Before all the people had reached the *sipapu* they cut down the bamboo; the joints in bamboo are caused by the people who were originally trapped inside. Despite the precautions some Two-Hearts succeeded in reaching the upperworld. Another version describes a raft construced of hollow reeds which the people used to ride out the flood.

At the time of emergence this world was occupied only by *Masau*, a deity. According to some versions *Masau* himself assisted the people through the *sipapu*. In others the first contact with *Masau* was made by the shrike who acted as an intermediary. In any case *Masau* gave the Hopis permission to settle in his land and marked off the boundaries of the territory they were to occupy.

AFTERWORLD

At death the hair of the deceased is washed in yucca suds and prayer feathers are placed on the hands, feet and in the hair. Over the face is placed a mask of cotton which is representative of the cloud mask the spirit will wear when it returns with the cloud people to bring rain to the village. Women are wrapped in their wedding robes; men are buried in a special blanket of diamond twill weave with a plaid design.

The ghosts of the dead are feared rather than death itself. To prevent the ghosts from returning to bother the living, *pahos* are given to the spirits of the deceased, and the trail back to the village from the burial site is ceremonially closed with sacred meal. Those who did the actual burial are purified with juniper smoke.

Four days after burial the spirit leaves the body and climbs out of the grave by means of a digging stick, which was placed there to serve as a ladder, and begins the journey to the Land of the Dead. The entrance to the Underworld is through the *Sipapu*, the Place of Emergence, in the Grand Canyon. *Kwanitaqa*, the One Horned God who can read a person's thought by looking into his heart, guards the Underworld. He forces Two-Hearts (evil persons) to take a slow, difficult trail, fraught with dangers, to reach the Land of the Dead. Persons who have followed the Sun Trail hurry along a path of sacred meal to reach the village of the Cloud People where their departed relatives wait for them.

The Two-Hearts meet their ends in fire pits where they are thrown, later to emerge as black beetles.

fallen into sinful ways, the priests sought the aid of animals and birds. They had heard the footsteps of someone walking above and decided to ask permission to ascend to the next world.

After several attempts by different birds the shrike found the opening that led to the upperworld. To reach the *sipapu*, the place of emergence, the help of the chipmunk was sought. Chipmunk planted a series of trees and sang magic songs over them in an effort to make them grow tall enough to reach the opening discovered by the shrike. Neither the spruce nor pine trees grew tall enough, but a bamboo finally grew up through the hole. Chipmunk then chewed an opening at the base of the reed to admit the pas-

The spirits of children who die before they are initiated are believed to return to the mother's house to be born again.

PRINCIPAL DEITIES

The Hopi pantheon includes between thirty and forty deities ranging in importance from culture heroes to major gods. There are often considerable differences in the functions and appearances of these deities among the various Hopi villages. The myths relating to the gods are sometimes vague or may differ greatly from one mesa to the next.

Sotuqnangu, the God of the Sky, is considered by most Hopis to be the most important deity. Some refer to him as the Supreme Being although he exercises no control over the other deities except for the Twin War Gods. Others call him Creator of the Earth, for, according to one myth, he created a virgin whom he later transformed into the earth. *Sotuquangu* is depicted wearing a single horn which represents male lightning. His eyes are cloud symbols. He is in charge of the heavens, lightning and clouds, and sends rain to make the plants grow. Sometimes he is referred to as the Star God and Lightning God.

Masau is both the God of the Earth and God of Death. It was *Masau* who permitted the Hopis to settle in his domain. He is depicted as a giant of a man and black in color. Although believed to be handsome, *Masau* always wears a terrifying mask, covered with blood, whenever he has contact with people. He is thought of as a fertility god of man and animals and is also associated with fire. In some legends he plays the part of a trickster.

Christian converts among the Hopi identify *Masau* with Satan declaring that he led the Hopi to practice a false religion. To strengthen their argument they offer an old legend which describes *Masau* as having a long tail which he cut off because it terrified children.

Mui-ingwa or *Alosaka*, the God of Germination, is also called the Two Horned God or Germ God. *Alosaka* lives underground and is concerned primarily with the propagation of plant life. He is often depicted with wings and is thought by some to be responsible for the fertility of the sky and earth. He was created by *Huru-ing Wuuti* along with his female counterpart, Sand Altar Woman, who is associated with childbirth.

Huru-ing Wuuti is thought of as the Mother of the Universe. As the Goddess of Hard Substances (turquoise, shell and coral), she is associated with wealth. Ugly by day and beautiful by night, she is visited daily by the sun in her kiva which is lo-

Masao Kachinas perform at Oraibi. This picture was taken in 1910 before photography was banned at dances by the Hopis.

cated in the western ocean. She is credited most frequently with being the Creator of the World and is said to own the stars and moon.

Kwanitaqa is the One Horned God who guards the entrance to the Underworld and determines which trail the spirits of the dead will follow to reach the land of the Cloud People.

Tawa, the Sun God or Father Sun, is thought of as the Giver of Life who acts as a special emissary for *Sotuqnangu*. *Tawa* travels daily to visit *Huru-ing Wuuti*. The Sun God has special powers which may be sought in ceremonials relating to both war and fertility. A morning prayer and an offering of corn meal are made to the sun daily by most Hopis. Newborn children are "presented" to the sun on the eighth day. *Tawa* is especially honored at the Winter Solstice ceremony to bring him back from his northward journey.

Kokyang Wuuti, Spider Woman, is depicted as a wise, kind, old woman who is always ready to help the Hopi people. Each village has a shrine to this deity who is believed to be present everywhere. She is the mother of the Twin War Gods. In some legends Spider Woman plays a major role in creating mankind; in others she is thought of as the creator of only those people who were not Hopis.

Po-okang-hoya and *Palo-ngao-hoya* are the Twin War Gods created by Spider Woman who is their grandmother. According to some legends they are responsible for keeping the world turning and preventing *Palolokon* from causing earthquakes. They are helpful to the Hopi people but are not above playing tricks on them on occasion.

Palolokon, the Water Serpent, is probably related to the Plumed Serpent, *Quetzacoatl*, of Mexico. It is believed to inhabit the waters under the earth and uses springs and lakes as windows

When Tahaum Soyoko, *the Ogre kachina, visits the village, children who have misbehaved are quickly persuaded to improve their conduct.*

to watch people. When displeased it may cause floods and earthquakes so this deity is one which must be placated. All moisture—sap, blood, and water—is in *Palolokon's* control.

Mu-yao, the Moon God, is seen as an old man who provides light at night. In the emergence legend Spider Woman made the moon by weaving a white cotton robe and placing it in the sky.

Ong-Wuuti, Salt Woman, inhabits the Salt Lake south of Zuni. *Pahos* (prayer feathers) are offered to her by Hopis who journey there to gather salt.

KACHINAS

Kachinas are not gods, but the symbolic representations, in human form, of the spirits of plants, animals, birds, places or ancestors. Since it is only the spirit that is depicted, there is no attempt at realism in the portrayals.

Kachinas at one time lived with the Hopis after their emergence from the Underworld and brought them rain with their dances, but the people became disrespectful so the kachinas left them and went off to live by themselves. Before they departed, however, they agreed to teach the people how to perform their rituals.

A kachina impersonator is believed to receive the spirit of the kachina he depicts when he wears its mask. Through him as an intermediary, the prayers of the villagers are conveyed to the more important deities.

Classifying kachinas is a pastime of students of Pueblo religion but not of the Indians themselves. They find it of no more importance to the practice, or understanding, of their religious beliefs than Christians would find a similar pigeon-holing of their numerous saints.

All Pueblo tribes have kachinas and kachina ceremonies, but the Hopis and Zunis have the largest number. The Hopis have about thirty *mong* or "chief" kachinas who appear to perform specific annual ceremonies; in addition to these are about 220 other kachinas who may appear during the kachina season. If a particular kachina performance does not bring the desired results, it may be abandoned entirely. New kachinas may also be added at any time.

Kachina performance in a kiva. Spectators are seated on a raised platform behind the ladder. Ray Naha

MAJOR CEREMONIES

WUWUCHIM

Wuwuchim is an annual initiation ceremony in which the Emergence from the Underworld is reenacted. During the rites all trails and roads into the village are ceremonially closed with sacred meal except the one leading from the burial ground. Lights and fires are extinguished and the spirits of the dead are invited to return to their village. *Masau* officiates at the initiation and ceremonially kindles a new fire which is then distributed to all households in the village. No outside visitors are permitted to attend the *Wuwuchim* which is held in November.

SOYAL

Shortly after the *Wuwuchim* the *Soyal* kachina appears in the village. His walk is unsteady and he sings in a quiet voice. Some believe this is because he has just awakened from the prolonged sleep all kachinas take after the *Niman;* others say the halting movements are childlike and symbolic of being reborn.

Soyal is the winter solstice ceremony held in December. The main purpose of the ceremony is to bring the sun back from its northward journey. It is also a time for purification and blessing rites to mark the rebirth of another year. Numerous *pahos* are made during the *Soyal* for houses, animals, plants, people and objects. It is during this time that the kivas are ritually opened to mark the beginning of the kachina season.

SOCIAL DANCES

Much social dancing is indulged in during January. Butterfly dances, adapted from the Rio Grande pueblos' Tablita dances, are performed. Outrageous caricatures of Navajos, Apaches, Spaniards (or any other group the impersonators wish to mimic) travel to each others' villages to perform. Buffalo dances, perhaps the only ones with any religious significance performed during this season, are also given. The buffalo is believed to bring the snow which is so necessary for successful spring planting.

POWAMU

Powamu, commonly called the Bean Dance, is the first major ceremony of the kachina season and includes the appearance of a number of *Mong* or Chief kachinas. (Prior to this, night kachina dances have been performed in the kivas.) It is at this ceremony that the greatest variety and number of kachina performers may be observed. Beans are planted in boxes of moist sand and forced to grow in the kivas where constant fires create a hothouse atmosphere.

An initiation for children into either the *Pow-amu* or Kachina society is also performed during the sixteen-day *Powamu* ceremony. The children are ritually whipped and afterwards learn that the kachina dancers are really human impersonators.

The *Powamu* dancers perform in the kiva to bless the bean sprouts. If the beans have grown tall a good harvest is predicted for the coming summer. Early the following morning the bean sprouts are distributed throughout the village and the children receive presents—plaques, kachina dolls, bows and arrows, rattles, moccasins—from the kachinas.

Powamu is also a time for the *Soyoko* kachinas to visit the homes of naughty children. These ugly monsters threaten to carry off and eat the youngsters if their behavior does not improve. The parents often must ransom the children with food. The sight of these terrifying ogres is enough to make anyone, young or old, improve his conduct.

PACHAVU

Every four years *Pachavu* is held during *Powamu*. The observance includes a spectacular parade in which innumerable kachinas appear in beautiful costume, many carrying huge plaques covered with bean sprouts. The procession moves about the village picking up new kachinas all the time; each sings his own songs and dances his own particular steps.

Periodically, and without warning, *Hu* or whipper kachinas appear and chase the spectators indoors to prevent viewing of certain rites. *Pachavu* ends with the distribution of the bean sprouts to the villagers.

PALOLOKON

Palolokon, or Water Serpent Ceremony (not an annual affair), is given about the same time of the *Powamu*. For pure theatrics the performance is unsurpassed. As the impersonators approach the kiva the light is extinguished; in a matter of minutes the room is once again illuminated to reveal an elaborate screen that stretches almost from wall to wall. On the floor, in front of the sun shield covers on the screen, are placed tiny corn shoots stuck in cones of clay. To the accompaniment of roaring sounds the sun shields lift and the heads of huge plumed and horned serpents appear. Snakelike they sway farther and farther into the room while *Koyemsi* sing. With violent motions they sweep away the miniature cornfield. *Hahai-wuuti*, the Mother of All Kachinas, approaches the serpents with a tray of corn meal and "nurses" each serpent. The Mudheads then

Qöqöle distributing presents during Powamu. T. Talaswaima

Niman Dance performed by the Hemis Kachinas and Kachin-manas. Ray Naha

attempt to push the serpents back under the sun shields but the snakes resist. The action and the roaring increase in intensity as the Mudheads wrestle with the *Palolokon*. The serpent figures give the impression of having tremendous strength and send the *Koyemsi* tumbling. Finally the serpents are forced back and the shields are closed; the kiva is darkened momentarily while the screen is dismantled and the performers depart.

The purpose of the Water Serpent ceremony is to honor the giant reptiles who control the waters of the earth. If the unpredictable creatures can be placated the people will receive the moisture they need for their crops and the springs, upon which the villages depend, will not fail.

KACHINA DANCES

Kachina Dances are held out-of-doors after the weather becomes milder, usually in April. Permission to stage a dance is given by the village chief; the sponsor of the dance determines which kachina will be presented and the day of the performance. Much time is spent by the impersonators in learning the songs which will be sung in the day-long presentation and in preparing the masks and other necessary equipment.

The purpose of a kachina dance is multifold;

the bringing of clouds and rain is of prime importance, but a successful dance also promotes harmony in the universe and ensures health, long life and happiness for the people. It is believed that the prayers of the people will be conveyed by the kachinas to the gods.

NIMAN

Niman, or Home Dance, is a sixteen-day ceremonial that begins shortly before the summer solstice and ends in mid-July. The dance held then marks the final performance of the kachina season and the kachinas return to their homes on the San Francisco Peaks until next *Soyal*.

Almost any kachina may be impersonated at the *Niman* but the *Hemis*, with its elaborate tablita, is usually the preferred one. The dance follows the usual kachina dance form, but between each round the kachinas distribute gifts to those present.

Clowns, (*Koyemsi, Koshares* or *Tcukus*), appear between dances to entertain the spectators with skits and games, often ribald in nature. Always the source of great amusement, they sometimes mimic the antics of whites or villagers whose behavior has not been proper.

Since the *Niman* coincides with the early harvest, corn and melons are distributed to the villagers and spectators. Bread, piki and native foods are also tossed to the crowd. Children receive rattles, dolls, bows and arrows, and bullrushes which are chewed like gum. Captive eagles also receive tiny plaques, miniature bows and arrows and a flat kachina doll.

The day after the *Niman* dance the kivas are ritually closed and the eagles, which have been held captive since their capture in early spring, are smothered. The feathers are removed from the birds for use in *pahos* and the bodies buried with the same attention and ceremony that is given to deceased members of the tribe.

FLUTE CEREMONY

The Flute Ceremony is performed biennially by the Gray Flute and Blue Flute Societies. The usual explanation for the ritual is that it brings

Hopi Niman Dance. 1910

the late summer rains that are needed to bring the crops to full maturity. The ceremony is much more complex than this, however, for in addition to the rain-bringing function (which is part of almost every ceremonial performed by the Pueblo Indians), the Flute ritual is a reenactment of the emergence and migration myths.

During the sixteen-day ceremonial elaborate Flute altars are set up in the clan houses (rather than the kivas) and initiation rites for new society members are conducted. An important part of the ritual includes a commemoration of the creation of the sun, and the participants in the public performance wear sun shields on their backs.

On the sixteenth day spectators may attend the final rites which begin with the blessing of the village spring. Then members of the Gray Flute

Society followed by the Blue Flute Society proceed to the village, each led by a priest and two Flute Maidens who carry small reed rings on slender rods.

On the way to the plaza the leader draws a cloud symbol on the ground with corn meal and the Flute Maidens, using the rods, toss the rings onto them; an act symbolic of the migrations (and the stops made along the way) of the Hopis. In some villages this rite is performed in the plaza.

When both societies are assembled in the plaza the Gray Flute leader and his water carrier enter the *kisi* (a temporary shelter of cottonwood branches) to pray while the songs of the Emergence are sung by the chorus to the sound of reed flutes. At the end of the prayers water from the carrier's gourd is poured into the *sipapu* (symbolic of the opening in the earth through which the Hopis emerged). The Blue Flute leader and his assistant then enter the *kisi* and offer more prayers and the ceremony ends after they emerge.

The flute is used in this ceremony to imitate the sound of locusts, an insect associated with summer; since warm days and additional rains are needed to mature the crops, it is an attempt to prolong the summer growing season.

SNAKE DANCE

Alternating with the biennial Flute Ceremony is the Snake Dance, probably the most widely known of all Hopi ceremonies. Although it is one of the Hopi rituals of lesser importance it attracts the biggest crowds of spectators—made up largely of curiosity seekers who are fascinated by the idea of humans handling live snakes.

The Snake Dance, like the Flute Dance, is a sixteen-day ceremonial and is believed to be one of the most ancient of all Pueblo rituals. There is evidence that this ceremony was once performed in most of the Rio Grande pueblos in pre-Spanish times. Today it survives only in the Hopi villages.

The ceremony itself is based on a legend concerning a young Hopi man who attempted to find the source of all waters by following the Colorado River to its headwaters. In a journey fraught with dangers he was assisted by Spider Woman.

Eventually he met the Great Snake who controlled the waters of the world from his kiva. The young man was initiated into the Snake tribe and was taught their ceremonies. Before he returned to his own people he married a young girl who had been transformed into a snake. (All reptiles are believed to be descended from the original offspring of this couple.)

During a serious drought Spider Woman

gave the young man the power to bring rain and designated him Antelope Chief, charged with the responsibility of teaching the wisdom and ceremonies of the Snake People to the Hopis.

The gathering of snakes by the Snake men begins eight days before the public performance. Four days are spent in hunting—one day in each of the cardinal directions. All snakes encountered, poisonous and non-poisonous, are blessed and gathered. Special altars are set up and sandpaintings are made in the kivas where the Snake and Antelope Societies conduct secret rites during the entire sixteen days. Each day the snakes are taken to the Snake kiva where they are carefully tended. All of the reptiles are washed and purified while the priests smoke and pray over them.

At sunrise of the eighth day the Antelope Race is held. Runners of all ages race from far below the mesa to the village on top. The winner receives prayer plumes and a gourd of sacred water to place in his cornfield.

Later in the day a *kisi* (the cottonwood shelter the young Hopi built each night for his Snake bride) is constructed in the plaza. A *sipapu* is dug in front of the *kisi* and then covered with a board.

In the late afternoon the Antelope men with grey-painted bodies appear followed by the Snake Dancers who are reddish brown in color.

The two groups each form lines facing each other—the Antelope men singing and the Snake men dancing—both lines moving forward and back.

The *kisi* is circled four times with each dancer stamping on the board over the *sipapu* to establish communication with the spirits of the Underworld. The Antelope and Snake men pair off for the dancing; the Antelope member reaches into the *kisi* and brings out a cornstalk which he carries in his mouth while making a circuit of the plaza. Each pair completes a circuit with the Antelope man handling the cornstalk as though it were a reptile.

Both groups then separate and encircle the *kisi* four more times before departing.

The next morning the Snake Race is held following the same course as the previous day. The Pueblo men pride themselves on their running ability and the uphill race proves their stamina beyond any doubt.

Late in the afternoon, after the customary four circuits of the *kisi,* the two societies gather again to form two facing lines in the plaza. The

Palolokon or Water Serpent Ceremony. Ray Naha

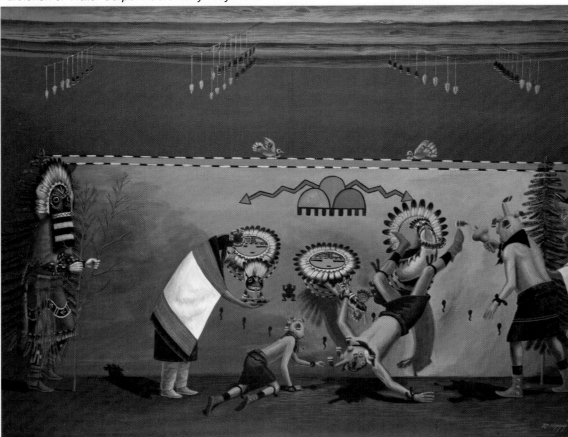

Carving in cottonwood depicts a Snake Dancer and a "hugger" or "guard" who distracts the serpent during the performance. In the foreground a Snake Priest uncoils a rattler by stroking it with his eagle feather wand.

lines dance back and forth; the Antelope men, with arms linked, sing and shake their flat mushroom-shaped leather rattles.

This time the Snake men pair off; one dancer reaches into the *kisi* and brings forth a snake. His partner, or "hugger," dances close behind and distracts the reptile with his eagle feather snake whip. One circuit is made with each snake until all have been danced with. A circle of corn meal is then inscribed on the ground and the snake gatherers throw their armfuls of reptiles into it. Before they can escape the Snake men grab them and race down the mesa to return them to their homes where, it is hoped, they will act as messengers and carry the Hopis' prayers for rain to the spirits of the Underworld.

The performers then drink an emetic which causes vomiting—an act of purification.

Occasionally snake handlers are bitten by poisonous reptiles but the Hopis have a snake medicine which they rub on the wound that protects them against the effects of the poison.

WOMEN'S DANCES

The *Marau, Lakon* and *Oaqol* Societies hold their rituals in the fall after the Snake or Flute ceremonies and before the *Wuwuchim*.

The ceremonies closely duplicate those given by the men's societies, with weather control, fertility, and curing being the primary purposes.

The *Lakon* ritual is often called a basket dance. The performers form a semi-circle to sing and dance. At the end of each song they throw gifts to the men who engage in a noisy free-for-all to grab the prize. Baskets are the most sought-after gifts but just as much enthusiasm goes into obtaining an ear of corn or a box of matches. Occasionally the gift is rendered totally unusable by the time a winner emerges.

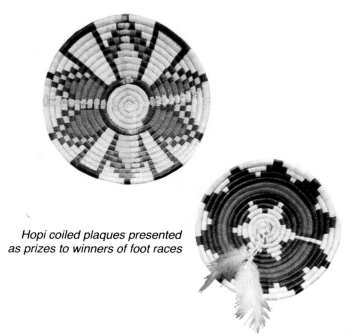

Hopi coiled plaques presented as prizes to winners of foot races

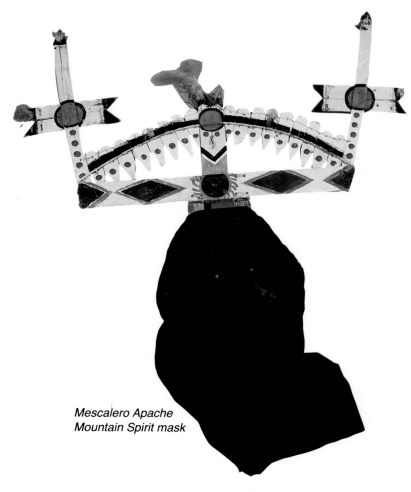

*Mescalero Apache
Mountain Spirit mask*

Apache

The Apache, who share a common linguistic and cultural background with the Navajo also share similar religious beliefs and ceremonies (most of which they adapted from the Pueblo tribes). Curing rituals and blessing rites which include, among other things, the use of sandpaintings, make up the bulk of Apache ceremonialism. As a general rule, however, the Apache have fewer ceremonies and these tend to be less complex than those of the Navajo.

DEITIES

Ysun, a supernatural force identified neither by sex nor location is the Creator of the Universe and looked upon as the Supreme Being. Referred to as "The Giver of Life," *Ysun* is the source of all power and has great influence over the affairs of people.

Everything on the earth, animate or inanimate, and in the sky is believed to have a spirit; the sun, moon, thunder, wind and lightning are especially powerful. Thunder Beings once lived with the peole and served as hunters by killing game with flint-tipped shafts of lightning. The earth itself is often referred to as Earth Woman but it is not personified.

White Painted Woman (the counterpart of the Navajo's Changing Woman) existed "from the beginning" and is the most important female deity. Child of Water and Killer of Enemies, whose mythological exploits are similar to those of the Navajo's Twin War Gods, are also important supernatural figures. Their relationship to White Painted Woman is not consistent among the various Apache bands and may be identified as sons, husbands or brothers. In one version of the creation myth Child of Water is described as creating man of mud or clouds.

A lesser but also important category of supernatural beings includes the Mountain People and Water People. The latter is made up of He Who Controls Water, a being who is dressed in a shirt of colored clouds and is responsible for the rains, and Water Monster, an unpleasant creature in

Western Apache Mountain Spirit Dancers. Ray Naha

serpent or human form which inhabits lakes and springs and causes the drowning of animals and people.

The Mountain People are the more important beings in this grouping. Called *Gan* (and similar to the Navajo *Yei* or Hopi *Kachina*) these supernaturals are identified with the specific mountain tops and caves which they inhabit. Like the Thunder Beings they too once lived with ordinary people but wishing to avoid the death that humans must eventually face, they left to seek a world of eternal life.

Coyote, in his usual role as troublemaker, is held responsible for bringing to man such undesirable things as death, gluttony, thievery, adultery and lying.

MOUNTAIN SPIRIT DANCE

Today the most important and elaborate ceremony given by the Apache is the girls' puberty rite. It is the only one they still have in common with their Athabascan-speaking relatives in Canada. According to their mythology it was White Painted Woman who taught this important ritual to the Apaches and it is she with whom the young women identify during this summer ceremony.

Coming-out parties are expensive affairs in any society and the Apache are no exception. The family of the young debutante must hire a shaman (either male or female) to conduct the ceremony, provide payment for the *Gan* impersonators and furnish huge quantities of food for the large number of friends and visitors who will

Apache medicine man prepares the staff carried by the young girl during her puberty ceremony

WESTERN WAYS

gather to attend the rituals and take part in the related social events.

On the first day a tipi is constructed of four spruce saplings to house the young girl and her older female attendant. The girl is dressed in ceremonial garments made of buckskin which have been painted yellow, the color of sacred pollen. The costume is a duplicate of the one worn by White Painted Woman, decorated with symbols of the moon, sun and stars. The long fringe represents sunbeams.

The girl is believed to possess special curative powers at this time of her life and may treat the sick and afflicted by touching or massaging. Between the lengthy chants sung by the shaman (during which the girl dances on a buckskin placed in the tipi) she attends all who come to her for aid.

Many taboos must be observed by the young lady, for her future depends on her disposition and deportment during the four-day ritual. She is cautioned about smiling or laughing because this would result in premature wrinkling. The ceremony is symbolic of the life journey the girl will take. If all goes well she will enjoy a long, happy and healthful life on the "pollen path."

On each of the four nights, impersonators of the *Gan*—the Mountain Spirits—will perform to bless the encampment and drive away any evil which may disrupt the proceedings. During this time the Mountain Spirit Dancers (often referred to incorrectly as Devil or Crown Dancers) also possess powers to cure and may treat patients by blowing away the sickness. The *Gan* are popular with the Apache and there is much rivalry among dance groups. In early times the *Gan* dancers often appeared to protect the bands from impending disasters such as epidemics. Now their appearances are limited to puberty rites and public exhibitions.

The dancers, who may number anywhere from four to sixteen plus one or more clowns, are painted under the direction of the shaman. At dusk they enter the dance ground, first approaching both the central fire and ceremonial tipi four times as a blessing.

A chorus, which carries the refrain to the verses sung by the medicine man, and a drummer accompany the dancers. The song determines which dance step will be used—short, high or free. Aside from the basic step restriction, each dancer performs as an individual. The dance itself

Gan dancers at an Apache girl's puberty ceremony. Duke Sine

is characterized by short, jerky, angular movements, and much posturing and gesturing with painted swordlike wands of yucca.

The dancers perform at intervals throughout each night. In between times the crowd participates in Round Dances—a form of social dancing identical with the Squaw Dances of the Navajo.

At the end of four days the tipi is ceremonially dismantled and the visitors depart. The family remains at the campground until the ninth day, on which the girl is purified by a bath in yucca suds. She then assumes the role of a marriageable woman.

Tohono O'otam sandpainting used in curing "wind sickness" (arthritis or paralysis)

Tohono O'otam*

O'OTAM ORIGIN MYTH

The origin myth, which takes an experienced storyteller four nights to complete, varies considerably in detail among the four dialect divisions of the O'otam. The version given here, which shares many similarities with Pueblo emergence legends, is a mere outline of the full story.

In the beginning there was only a darkness in which Earthmaker and Buzzard drifted.

Earthmaker rubbed dirt from his skin and

*As of 1986 the Papago have officially changed their tribal name back to the original name—Tohono O'otam.

held it in his hand; out of it grew a greasewood bush. From a ball of gum taken from the bush, Earthmaker then created the world. As the earth was being joined to the sky, *I'itoi*, another supernatural, came into being. Coyote, who served as a messenger for the deities, also appeared about the same time.

The newly formed universe was a wobbly affair until the Spider People sewed the earth and the sky together. Buzzard formed mountains and water courses with his wings and Earthmaker created the stars, sun and moon.

The first attempt to create life resulted in such imperfect human beings that the supernaturals brought about a flood to destroy them. Before the flood Earthmaker, *I'itoi* and Coyote agreed that the first to appear afterwards would be known as Elder Brother. *I'itoi* emerged first and assumed the title.

Elder Brother then formed new human beings from clay but this led to a conflict with Earthmaker who, in anger, disappeared underground.

I'itoi dwelt with his creations (identified as the *Hohokam*) and taught them how to live in the desert and gave them ceremonies necessary to bring rain. Hostility between *I'itoi* and the people broke out and they decided to kill him. In four years *I'itoi* revived with the help of winds and went underground to secure aid from people

Ceremonial "rain house" at Santa Rosa Village

Baskets and jars used in making saguaro wine. Basket on the right contains saguaro fruit. Plaited palm frond basket (left) is used as a strainer. Center basket and small basket cup are used to serve the liquor.

there. These were the Pima and the O'otam and they agreed to help *I'itoi.*

Gopher burrowed through the ground to lead the people out of the four Underworlds. With *I'itoi's* assistance they drove out the *Hohokam. I'itoi* then helped the Pima and the O'otam to establish themselves in the desert. The boundaries for each group were marked by corn kernels carried by the winds. *I'itoi* then left and returned to live underground in the vicinity of Baboquivari Peak.

CURING RITES

Most human disease is believed to be caused by animals which have been treated disrespectfully or injured. The *Makah,* or medicine men, have the power to diagnose the cause and the patient then goes to a singer who possesses the power and fetishes to effect a cure.

Rattlesnakes can cause stomach aches; sore feet might be caused by horned toads. Offending a turtle could result in a crippled leg and a deer which had been injured could bring rheumatism to its tormenter. Each malady requires a series of songs to cure it. In case the disease is traced to an animal introduced by the Spaniards, the recitations of a rosary might be prescribed.

AFTERWORLD

Disposal of the corpse took place soon after death as the ghosts of the deceased were greatly feared. Formerly burial was made in a rock crevice and covered with stones or in a stone cairn roofed with logs. Food and possessions were placed with the body in the grave to accompany the spirit on its four-day journey to the Underworld "somewhere" in the east. The afterworld was believed to be a place of much rain and plenty of food.

Today annual offerings of food and drink are made at the graves of the deceased on All Souls Day, a practice picked up from the Mexicans but not unlike the native custom.

O'OTAM CEREMONIES

Although most O'otam have long been converted to various Christian sects, a number of the old ceremonials are still performed.

O'otam ceremonialism is a mixture of hunting and agricultural rituals. The most important aspect of each rite is the bringing of life-sustaining rain to the land. Any successfully conducted ritual (inter-village races and games, salt pilgrimages to the Gulf of Lower California, dances, curing and puberty rites and ceremonies performed at local shrines) would bring rain.

Tcirkena Dance. Mike Chiago

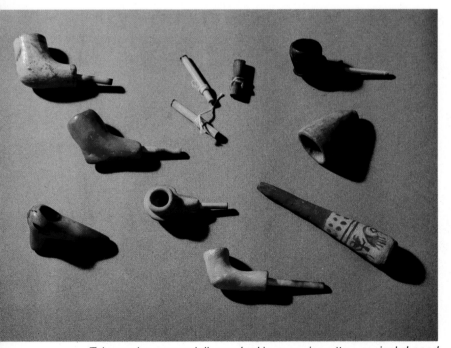

Tobacco is ceremonially smoked in cane cigarettes, conical shaped "cloud blowers," and short elbow pipes. The long stemmed peace pipes or calumets were not used in the Southwest. Upper left, Tesuque. Four lower left, Hopi. Upper right, pipe and cloudblower, Navajo. Lower right, cloudblower, Mojave.

SAGUARO WINE FESTIVAL

Late in June when the fruit of the giant saguaro ripens the O'otam conduct a wine festival, a ceremony taught them by *I'itoi*. The use of fermented beverages for religious purposes is a custom that was common in Mexico and unknown north of O'otam country in pre-Spanish times.

In the old days agriculture provided the Desert People with food for only part of the year; the rest of the time they had to depend on hunting and gathering. The saguaro provided them with fresh fruit, syrup and a cake made from the seeds.

The syrup-making process produces a juice which is allowed to ferment for three days in the "rain house" under the care of the "Keeper of the Smoke," the village headman and ceremonial leader. Rain songs are sung while the liquid ferments and men and women dance at night. As a part of the fertility ritual, sexual license was formerly permitted but not any more.

At noon of the third day the headmen

gathered to recite long poems over the baskets of wine. The men of the village sat in a circle and passed the baskets around until they were drained. The drinking of wine, like the smoking of tobacco, was considered a ceremonial duty and was not formerly indulged in for mere pleasure.

The planting of crops takes place after the wine festival to make use of the rains that are bound to follow.

Today many families also prepare saguaro wine for their own use at this time but the custom to "cover the wine with a song" continues and anyone who accepts a drink of the liquor recites a poem which invariably relates to clouds or rain.

TCIRKWENA DANCE

Formerly it was customary for villages to challenge one another to games, contests or dances. One dance, Tcirkwena, still performed on occasion, is referred to variously as a Skipping Dance, a Season Dance or a Winter Rain Dance.

The series of eight songs required for these dances were "dreamed" by a singer. This man would then train young boys and girls to perform the dance steps. During the dance they carried effigies of birds, clouds or rainbows made of cotton.

Musical accompaniment was provided by basket drums, rasping sticks and a chorus of older men who had learned the song series.

The village which hosted the dancers considered the ceremony as a blessing which assured them of sufficient rainfall. The older women of the village might honor the visitors by dancing alongside them.

After the performances the guests were given a feast and gifts in payment.

CHICKEN PULL

Corso de gallo, or the Chicken Pull, is a game that was introduced into the Southwest along with the horse by the Spaniards. It is a contest of riding skill, traditionally performed on San Juan's Day (June 24). It may be given at other times as a separate event or in connection with a native ceremonial.

The O'otam version of the Chicken Pull takes place on a sandy race track several hundred feet long. Halfway down the track a live rooster is buried up to its neck in the loose sand. Individual riders galloping past lean out of their saddles and attempt to pull the rooster out of the ground. The rooster frantically dodges the grasping fingers and it usually takes many tries before a rider succeeds in wrenching the luckless fowl free.

A general free-for-all follows with all riders trying to grab the rooster and the successful contestant beating off his attackers by swinging the chicken as a club. The "game" ends with the disintegration of the rooster.

Most tribes which adopted the Chicken Pull have given it some religious connotation. Among the Rio Grande pueblos it has an agricultural significance with the "planting" and subsequent removal of the rooster regarded as symbolic of sowing and reaping. The blood and feathers of the fowl and the foam and sweat of the lathered horses represent rain and clouds and are also considered to be a blessing for the earth which promotes fertility.

Among the O'otam the rainmaking significance was probably the main consideration, for locally San Juan's Day is still traditionally thought of as a day of rain.

Chicken Pull. Henry Enos

Yaqui Deer Dancer

Yaqui

The Yaqui's native religion was greatly changed by the introduction of Catholicism by Jesuit missionaries in the arly 1600s. As enthusiastic converts they soon observed a full Roman Catholic ceremonial calendar. Church rituals were not led by ordained priests but by Yaqui men known as *maestros* who conducted services in a combination of Spanish, Yaqui and Latin. Even today the Yaqui churches are totally independent of the Roman Catholic Church.

Easter Season

The most elaborate ceremonies conducted in the Yaqui settlements of southern Arizona occur during Lent. These include the Yaqui version of the Catholic liturgy for the Lenten season and Easter, and a Passion play. The basic theme presented is the triumph of good over evil.

The *Fariseo* (Pharisees) and *Caballero* societies are in charge of the Easter ceremony. Their members impersonate the enemies of Christ who pursued and persecuted Him. *Chapayekas,* the common soldiers of the *Fariseos,* wear grotesque masks of painted hide or paper and carry swords and daggers of wood. Judas is their saint. To prevent the evil he depicts from entering his heart, each *Chapayeka* must carry the cross of his rosary in his mouth while wearing his mask.

The *Matachin* society is a men's dance group under vow to Mary and is referred to as "soldiers of the Virgin." During the Easter ceremonies they are allied with the church group, led by the *maestros,* in opposition to the *Fariseos.* They wear headdresses decorated with paper flowers and ribbons and carry wands decorated with brightly colored feathers. The young boys wear white dresses and act as guardians of the Virgin. The dances this group performs, including a maypole dance, all appear to be of European origin.

On Holy Saturday the *Matachinas* successfully defend the church against attack by the *Fariseos* and "kill" the *Chapayekas* with a barrage of

Yaqui flute player and drummer

flowers. (Flowers play an important part in Yaqui services; they represent divine blessings and a protection against evil.) The masks and weapons of the *Chapayekas* are later burned on a pyre with a figure of Judas.

FIESTA DANCERS

The only remaining rituals of native origin are the performances of the *Pascola* and Deer dancers. They are ancient hunting ceremonials which dramatize this once-important activity. Although these impersonators take part in the church processions, most of their dancing takes place in a small ramada removed from the church building.

A chorus of three Deer Singers, who also play a water drum (a half gourd turned hollow side down in a bowl of water) and rasping sticks, sing ancient hunting chants which describe poetically the world of the deer. A fourth musician simultaneously plays a bamboo flute and beats a flat, hide-covered drum.

The *Pascolas*, "the old men of the fiesta," (ceremonial hosts of the fiesta) are aligned with

Bamboo wand and gourd rattle used by the Matachini dancers

Matachini Dancers.
The young man dressed in white is a guardian of the Virgin

Chapayekas march on the church with swords and daggers

the church when it is under attack by the *Fariseos*. During their own dances they act the part of clowns and entertain the spectators with jokes, pantomime and horseplay. The *Pascolas'* dance has a shuffling step which emphasizes the soft rustling sound of their cocoon leg rattles. A jangling beat is provided by a wood and metal rattle which is struck in the palm of one hand. When performing they wear a small wooden mask over the face; otherwise it is worn at the side of the head.

The Deer impersonator wears a deer head when dancing. Red ribbons representing flowers are wound about the horns. The original purpose of this dance was to so honor the deer that it would willingly allow itself to be caught by the hunters. The dance itself is a perfect pantomime of the deer's movements. More rapid and tense than the *Pascola's* dance, the Deer impersonator maintains a steady "roll" with his gourd rattles, pausing occasionally to posture in imitation of a living deer.

Pascola rattles (wood with brass disks) and belt with deer hoof tinklers

Chapayeka masks are placed on wooden swords next to the fiesta cross between dances. Custom requires the performer to lie on the ground either to remove or put on his mask.

A figure of Judas, the "saint" of the Fariseos, goes up in flames along with the masks and equipment of the Chapayekas in order to destroy the evil they have absorbed during the Easter ceremonies.

Peyote

Peyote *(Lophophora williamsii)* is a small, turnip-shaped, spineless cactus that grows in the lower Rio Grande valley from southern New Mexico southward to Nayarit, Mexico. It contains nine alkaloid substances, part of which, mainly mescaline, are hallucinogenic in nature; that is, they induce dreams or visions. Reactions to peyote seem to vary with the social situation under which it is used. In some it may merely cause nausea; believers may experience optic, olfactory and auditory sensations. Under ideal conditions color visions may be experienced and peyote may be "heard" singing or speaking. The effects wear off within twenty-four hours and leave no ill aftereffects. Peyote is non-habit forming.

The use of peyote in rituals began in pre-Columbian times in Mexico. The Spaniards record its use by the Aztec. It is still used today among a number of tribes including the Tarahumara, Huichol and Cora. Its purpose varies considerably, from use as a charm in footraces and hunting to a medicine in curing rites. It may also be employed to predict the weather or to locate lost objects (the revelations appear in

Dried peyote buttons and a "peyote bean" or "mescal bean" necklace. Use of the so-called "mescal bean" (actually the seed of a small evergreen tree, Sophora secundiflora, *and not the agave) preceded peyote in the Southern Plains region. Like peyote it contains alkaloids which cause similar physiological and psychological effects when eaten. Necklaces of these beans are often included in the kits of peyote users.*

peyote-induced visions). Peyote also appears in elaborate rainmaking ceremonies.

Peyote was first introduced into the southern Plains in the 1840s. The Lipan Apache, Comanche and Kiowa were the first tribes to adopt its use. Its first usage was primarily medicinal in nature; in the visions induced by peyote the patient made contact with supernatural powers which restored his health. Vomiting caused by nausea got rid of the sickness and left one spiritually purified.

Occasionally peyote was used in connection with warfare; it revealed the location of the enemy by means of a vision or by speaking to the user.

From the southern Plains the use of peyote spread eastward to the Great Lakes region and northward as far as southern Canada. As it spread to other tribes each group adapted peyote to fit its own cultural background. Following the suppression of the Ghost Dance religion during the early reservation era, the peyote cult gained many followers. The drastic and demoralizing changes caused by reservation life made the Indian people receptive to a new religious philosophy that gave them a sense of well being and pride and stressed the importance of the "Indianness" of the participants. It was a religion of hope for a beaten people and its followers benefited spiritually, physically and mentally.

It was at this time that the Native American Church had its beginnings. Drawing much from Christian teachings, it made use of peyote as a sacrament. The peyotists claim the whiteman had the Bible so that he could learn about God; the Indian was given peyote for the same purpose, and biblical passages (all references to herbs are construed to include peyote) were often quoted to justify its use.

The Native American Church stresses a high moral code which includes brotherly love, care of the family, self reliance and the avoidance of alcohol.

Incorporated in 1918, the N.A.C. claims over 200,000 followers today. Not all peyote users, however, are members of the church.

There has, of course, been much opposition to the peyote cults, most of it based on the misunderstanding of the effects peyote has on the mind and body. Lurid, though fictitious, details of sex orgies are often described by wishful thinkers among the anti-peyote forces. Some claim its use results in laziness, arrogance, addiction and deformed births (essentially the same dangers that were attributed to the use of tea and coffee when

Kiowa peyote equipment. The drum is made of a cast iron kettle with tripod legs. The rope, tied over marbles placed under the buckskin head, forms an intricate star pattern which represents Father Peyote. Deer antler tine is used in tightening the drum head. Other equipment includes drum stick, eagle bone whistle, beaded staff, gourd rattles and feather fans. Christian influence is seen in the frequent inclusion of rosaries and religious medals.

first introduced into Europe).

Although there is no federal law prohibiting the use of peyote (despite many attempts to pass such legislation), at least a dozen states and one tribe (Navajo) have passed laws outlawing its use. Several states and the Navajo tribe have since repealed the prohibition or allow the use of peyote as a sacrament. Arizona's anti-peyote law was declared unconstitutional in 1960.

Tribal members who follow their traditional religion are naturally upset over the introduction of a new religion and oppose it on grounds that it is "foreign." Many Christian sects working among Indians oppose peyote religion because it "misinterprets" Christian beliefs to accommodate the use of peyote. Despite this opposition—and often because of it—the peyote cults continue to grow.

NAVAJO PEYOTISM

Despite its early appearance in the Southwest the use of peyote among Navajo was unknown until the 1920s. Southern Ute medicine men who used peyote to treat Navajo patients were the first contacts they had with either the cactus or the cult. The success of peyote as a medicine in the treatment of their illnesses led many of them to follow the "Peyote Road."

Then, as now, many cult members continued to make use of traditional Navajo curing rites and, as with other tribal groups, modified the peyote ritual to fit their own cultural traditions.

The rapid spread of peyotism on the Navajo reservation in the late 1930s is attributed to the economic stresses caused by the government's stock reduction program. As their way of life appeared to be threatened, some Navajo found a sense of security in the peyote religion. The sudden increase in peyote users alarmed many traditionalists, government officials, and missionaries and resulted in official action by the Navajo tribal council. In 1940 the sale, use or possession of peyote on the Navajo reservation was declared an offense punishable by fine and/or imprisonment. Despite this prohibition the cult continued to grow. By 1950 an estimated nine to ten thousand Navajo were peyotists. In 1965 the number had grown to between twenty-five and thirty-five thousand and is still increasing today.

PEYOTE CEREMONY

There is no strict service that must be followed in conducting peyote ceremonies by either members of the Native American Church or non-affiliated peyotists.

Among the Navajo peyote users ceremonies may be given to bless a new house, celebrate a birthday or special holiday, solemnize a wedding, insure good health for children who are leaving for school, or cure an illness.

The meeting is usually sponsored by a family which arranges for a Road Chief to conduct the ceremony and to provide food and peyote buttons for guests.

The meeting, usually held in a hogan, though occasionally in a tipi, begins at sundown with the preparation of a crescent-shaped altar by the Road Chief and the kindling of a ritually laid fire by the Fire Chief. The altar represents the universe to some and the moon to others. A line drawn the length of the crescent is symbolic of the Peyote Road. In the middle of the altar, on a bed of sage, is placed Chief (or Father) Peyote, a button of unusual size.

Other opening rites include the blessing and purifying in cedar smoke of the peyote paraphernalia. Sage is also "smoked" and passed around to be rubbed on the hands and body as a medicine. Cigarettes are ritually smoked by all present, four puffs each to the Road Chief, Mother Earth and the participant as a blessing and prayer.

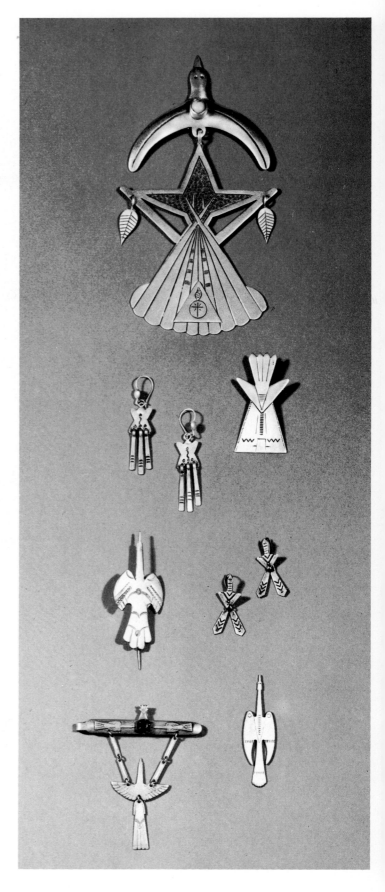

Peyote buttons are then passed around for the members to eat.

The Road Chief begins the singing with four opening songs followed by solo performances by the drummer and Cedar Chief, and later by other members.

Peyote jewelry made of German silver was first produced among Plains tribes about 1900. Similar work by Navajo smiths in sterling appeared in the early 1940s. The long-necked bird depicted in this jewelry is the anhinga, (commonly called a snake bird or water turkey), a cormorant-like bird of the Gulf Coast. Its feathers, which have a corrugated edge, are highly prized for peyote fans. The peyote bird carries the prayers of the worshipper to the supreme being. Top two pins and both pairs of earrings are Navajo. Three bottom pieces are Kiowa.

© RICHARD LEROY COLLECTION

Peyote Dream. Jerry Ingram

During the evening the fire is constantly attended by the Fire Chief whose duty it is to keep the fire and altar in order. During the course of the night he adds a "tail" of ash to the crescent altar transforming it into an eagle or a thunderbird.

At midnight the Road Chief sings another set of songs and water is brought in to be drunk. More cigarettes are smoked as prayers, started by the members and finished by the Road Chief, to assure that the prayers will be heard. The Road Chief then goes outside to blow an eagle bone whistle to call the spirits. Occasionally confessions or testimonials to the power of peyote may be given by those present.

If the ceremony is being conducted as a curing rite the Road Chief chews a peyote button and gives it to the patient to swallow. He also purifies the patient by fanning him with cedar smoke.

At first morning light water is again served by the Water Woman (sometimes called Peyote Woman) and the Road Chief sings his special morning water songs.

After the closing ceremony, which includes four more songs by the Road Chief, the ritual disposal of cigarette stubs, and final prayers, the people gather out-of-doors for a feast.

During the course of the evening an average of four buttons is consumed by each person present. The successful worshipper may see visions or hear peyote talk to him and instruct him on how to solve his problems or improve his life. If he is sick or depressed peyote may cure him. The evening is spent in contemplation and communion with God, with peyote serving as a sacrament. Occasionally cult members will eat a bit of peyote at other times as a prayer but generally the belief is held that peyote does not "work" outside of meetings. The companionship of fellow peyote members also enhances the sense of well-being resulting from the use of the peyote itself.

Calendar of Southwestern Indian Ceremonials

Dates given here are often approximate; ceremonies may be scheduled to fall on the nearest weekend to permit participation by tribal members who live or work in town. Many dances are unscheduled or are announced annually. Inquire locally for exact date and village if not given here.

NOTE: Recording, photographing, sketching or note-taking at Indian ceremonials generally is strictly forbidden. Those tribes that do not forbid it still require that written permission be obtained from the local Indian authorities. Please do not create unpleasant incidents by ignoring this restriction. For general conduct, a good rule of thumb to follow is simply this: anything you would not hesitate to do (or wear) in your own church, temple or synagogue is probably also permissible at an Indian ceremonial.

ARIZONA

Date	Event	Tribe and Location
Feb.—usually last three weekends	Powamu (Bean Dance)	Hopi—all villages
February through April	Night Kachina Dances	Hopi—all villages
Easter—from Ash Wednesday through Easter	Easter Ceremonies	Yaqui. Villages of Pascua, New Pascua and Barrio Libre (Tucson) and Guadalupe (Tempe)
April through July	Daytime Kachina Dances	Hopi—all villages
June 24	San Juan's Day—Chicken Pull	O'otam, Santa Rosa and other villages.
Late June or early July	Saguaro Wine Festival	O'otam. Various villages.
Middle to late July	Niman (Home Dance)	Hopi—all villages
July 30–31	San Ignacio's Day. Fiesta and dances.	Yaqui—Pascua
Middle to late August	Snake Dance	Hopi. Even years at Shipavlovi, Shungopavy and Hotevilla. Odd years at Mishongnovi and Walpi.
Middle to late August	Flute Dance	Alternate years in above villages.
August, third weekend	Peach Festival	Havasupai at Supai village
October 4 and prior week	Fiesta of Saint Francis	Yaqui and Papago pilgrimage to Magdalena, Sonora

NEW MEXICO

Date	Event	Tribe and Location
January 1	Tablita and Turtle Dances. Transfer of "canes of authority" to new officers.	Cochiti, San Juan, Taos, Zia
January 6	King's Day. Animal or Eagle dances in most Rio Grande pueblos. Blessing of "canes of authority" and installation of new officers.	Cochiti, Jemez, Sandia, San Juan, San Ildefonso, Tesuque, Taos, Zia.
January 23	Buffalo and Comanche Dances	San Ildefonso
February—entire month	Frequent dances in most Rio Grande pueblos.	Inquire locally for time and place.
February 2	Buffalo Dance	San Felipe
February 15	Buffalo Dance	San Juan
March 19	Fiesta and dances	Laguna
April 1	Spring Corn or Tablita Dances	Most pueblos
Easter	Tablita Dances. Races.	Most pueblos
May 1	Tablita Dance	San Felipe
May 3	Santa Cruz Day. Tablita Dance.	Taos
May 3	Tablita Dance and Coming of the River Men	Cochiti
June—first week	Corn Dance	Tesuque
June	Kachina Dances	Zuni
June 8	Buffalo Dance	Santa Clara
June 13	San Antonio's Day. Tablita or Buffalo Dances	Cochiti, Sandia, San Juan, Santa Clara, San Ildefonso, Taos.
June 24	San Juan's Day. Dances, races and Chicken Pulls at various pueblos.	Acoma, Cochiti, Santa Ana, Santo Domingo, Isleta, San Felipe, San Juan, Taos.
June 29	San Pedro's Day. Fiesta, dances and Chicken Pulls.	Acoma, Cochiti, Santa Ana, Santo Domingo, Isleta, Cochiti.
July 4	Nambe Ceremonial	Nambe Falls

July 4	Mescalero Apache Gan Dancers and Rodeo	Mescalero
July 14	San Buenaventura's Day. Tablita Dance.	Cochiti
July 25 and 26	Santiago's and Santa Ana's Day. Corn Dances and Rabbit Hunt.	Acoma, Cochiti, Laguna, Santa Ana, Taos.
Late July	Santa Clara Ceremonial at Puye Cliff dwellings.	Puye
August 2	Old Pecos Bull Dance	Jemez
August 4	Tablita Dance	Santo Domingo
August 10	San Lorenzo's Day. Fiesta and Corn Dances.	Picuris, Acomita, Laguna.
August 12	Santa Clara's Day Dances.	Santa Clara
August 15	Corn Dance	Zia
August 15	Harvest Dance	Launa (Mesita)
August 28	Fiesta	Isleta
September 2	Harvest Dance and Fiesta	Acoma
September 4	San Augustin's Day. Harvest Dance.	Isleta
September 8	Harvest Dance	Laguna (Encinal Village)
September 8	Corn Dance	San Ildefonso
September 19	Harvest Dance	Laguna
September 25	St. Elizabeth's Day. Corn Dances.	Laguna
September 29	Various dances	Taos
September 30	San Geronimo's Day. Pole climbing by Koshares. Races, Dances.	Taos
September—last week	Evergreen Dances. Harvest Dances.	Isleta (date announced annually) San Juan (date announced annually)
October 4	Elk Dance and Fiesta	Nambe
October 17	Corn Dance	Laguna (Paraje Village)
November 12	Corn Dance and fiesta.	Jemez
November 12	San Diego's Day. Animal Dances.	Tesuque
Late November or Early December	Shalako	Zuni
December 12	Matachine Dance	Jemez
December 24	Ceremonial Dances in mission churches. Processions.	Most pueblos
December 25	Various dances	Most pueblos
December 26	Turtle Dance	San Juan
December 26	Matachine Dance	Taos
December 31	Deer Dance	Sandia
Late December	Animal and other dances	Most pueblos

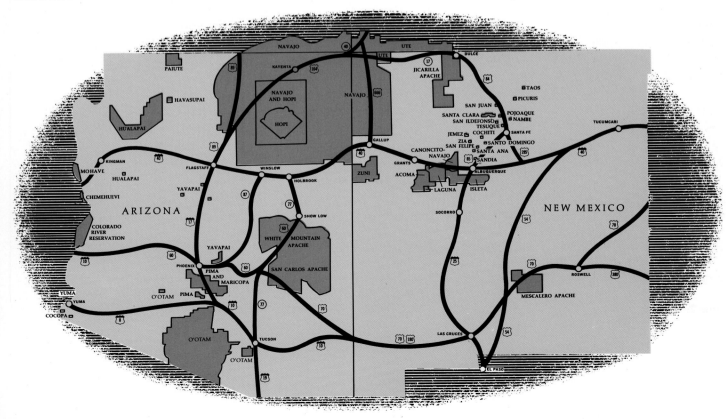

Suggested Reading

ABERLE, DAVID F. and OMER C. STEWART. *Navajo and Ute Peyotism: A Chronological and Distributional Study.* University of Colorado Studies. Series in Anthropology, 1957.

BAHTI, TOM. *Southwestern Indian Arts and Crafts.* KC Publications, [1964] 1983.

BAHTI, TOM. *Southwestern Indian Tribes.* KC Publications, [1968] 1982.

BENEDICT, RUTH. *Zuni Mythology.* 2 vols. Columbia University Press. New York, 1935.

BUNZEL, RUTH L. "Introduction to Zuni Ceremonialism." B.A.E. *Forty-seventh Annual Report,* 1929–30. Washington, D.C., 1932.

BUNZEL, RUTH L. "The Sia." B.A.E. *Eleventh Annual Report,* 1889–90. Washington, D.C., 1894.

BUNZEL, RUTH L. "The Zuni Indians." B.A.E. *Twenty-third Annual Report,* 1901–1902. Washington, D.C., 1904.

COLLIER, JOHN. *On the Gleaming Way.* Sage Books. Denver, 1962.

DOCKSTADER, FREDERICK J. *The Kachina and the White Man.* University of New Mexico Press, [1954] 1985.

DUTTON, BERTHA. *Sun Father's Way.* University of New Mexico Press, 1963.

FEWKES, J. W. "The Pa-lu-lu-kon-ti." *Journal of American Folklore,* VI. 1893.

FEWKES, J. W. "Tusayan Snake Ceremonies," B.A.E. *Sixteenth Annual Report, Part II.* Washington, D.C., 1897.

GIDDINGS, RUTH W. *Yaqui Myths and Legends.* University of Arizona Press. Tucson, 1959.

GONZALES, CLARA. *The Shalakos Are Coming.* Museum of New Mexico Press. Santa Fe, 1969.

GOODWIN, GRENVILLE. *The Social Organization of the Western Apache.* University of Arizona Press, 1969.

HAWLEY, FLORENCE. "The role of Pueblo social organization in the dissemination of Catholicism." *Amer. Anthropol.,* vol. 48. 1946.

HIGHWATER, JAMAKE. *Ritual of the Wind.* Viking Press. New York City, 1977.

KACZKURKIN, MINI VALENZUELA. *Yoeme.* Sun Tracks, Dept. of English, University of Arizona. Tucson, 1977.

KLUCKHOHN, CLYDE. *Navaho Witchcraft.* Beacon Press. Boston, 1944

KLUCKHOHN, CLYDE and DOROTHEA LEIGHTON. *The Navajo.* Harvard University Press, 1946.

LA BARRE, WESTON. *The Peyote Cult.* Schocken Books. New York, 1969.

LASKI, VERA. *Seeking Life.* American Folklore Society. Philadelphia, 1958.

OPLER, MORRIS E. *An Apache Life-Way.* University of Chicago Press, 1941.

MOON, SHEILA. *A Magic Dwells.* Wesleyan University Press. Middletown, Connecticut, 1974.

NEQUATEWA, EDMUND. *Truth of a Hopi.* Museum of Northern Arizona. Flagstaff, 1967.

PAINTER, MURIEL T. *Easter at Pascua Village.* University of Arizona Press. Tucson, 1960.

PAINTER, MURIEL T. *With Good Heart.* University of Arizona Press. Tucson, 1986.

PARSONS, E. C. *Hopi and Zuni Ceremonialism.* American Anthropological Association Memoirs, Vol. XXXIX. Menasha, 1933.

PARSONS, E. C. *A Pueblo Indian Journal, 1920–21.* American Anthropological Association Memoirs, Vol. XXXII. Menasha, 1925.

PARSONS, E. C. *Pueblo Indian Religion.* 2 vols. University of Chicago Press, 1939.

REICHARD, GLADYS A. *Navajo Religion.* University of Arizona Press. [1950] 1983.

ROEDIGER, VIRGINIA M. *Ceremonial Costumes of the Pueblo Indians.* University of California Press, 1961.

SLOTKIN, J. S. *The Peyote Religion.* The Free Press. Glencoe, Illinois, 1956.

TALAYESVA, DON. *Sun Chief: The Autobiography of a Hopi Indian.* Ed. by L. W. Simmons, Yale University Press, 1942.

TYLER, HAMILTON A. *Pueblo Gods and Myths.* University of Oklahoma Press, 1964.

UNDERHILL, RUTH M. *Papago Indian Religion.* (Columbia University Contributions to Anthropology, Vol. XXXIII.) Columbia University Press, 1946.

UNDERHILL, RUTH M. *Ceremonial Patterns in the Greater Southwest.* (American Ethnological Society Monographs, Vol. XIII.) J. J. Augustin. New York, 1962.

UNDERHILL, RUTH M. *Red Man's Religion.* The University of Chicago Press, 1965.

VOTH, H. R. *The Traditions of the Hopi.* Field Columbian Museum (Anthropological Series) Vol. VIII. Chicago, 1905.

WATERS, FRANK. *Masked Gods.* Ballentine Books. New York, 1950.

WATERS, FRANK. *Book of the Hopi.* Ballantine Books. New York, 1956.

WHITE, LESLIE A. "The Acoma Indians." B.A.E. *Forty-seventh Annual Report,* 1929–30. Washington, D.C., 1932.

WYMAN, LELAND C. *The Windways of the Navajo.* The Taylor Museum of the Colorado Springs Fine Arts Center, 1962.

POETRY

ASTROV, MARGOT. *American Indian Prose & Poetry* (formerly *Winged Serpent*). Capricorn Books. New York, 1962.

DAY, A. GROVE. *The Sky Clears.* University of Nebraska Press. Lincoln, 1964.

ROTHENBERG, JEROME (ed.). *Shaking the Pumpkin.* Doubleday and Company, Inc. Garden City, New York, 1972.

(These anthologies list numerous primary sources.)

MUSIC

Folkways/Scholastic Records, Englewood Cliffs, New Jersey.

Indian House Recordings, Taos, New Mexico.

Canyon Records, Phoenix, Arizona.

Taylor Museum, Colorado Springs, Colorado.

Published by KC Publications · Box 14883 · Las Vegas, NV 89114

Printed by Dong-A Printing Co., Ltd. · Seoul, Korea